Spler Sweaisn Recipes

Collected by Kerstin Olsson Van Gilder

On the cover: Sara Sofia Anderson

Edited by Michelle Nagle Spencer, Dorothy Crum,
Miriam Canter, Cheryl Ferguson, Mary Jo DeMeulenaere,
Joan Liffring-Zug, and John Zug

BOOKS BY MAIL Stocking Stuffers POSTPAID You may mix titles. One book for $8.95; two for $16; three for $23; four for $28; twelve for $75. Please send $2.50 for a complete catalog. *(Prices subject to change.)* Please call 1-800-728-9998

American Gothic Cookbook
Cherished Czech Recipes
Dandy Dutch Recipes
Dear Danish Recipes
Fine Finnish Foods
Great German Recipes
Intriguing Italian Recipes
Norwegian Recipes
Pleasing Polish Recipes
Quality Czech Mushroom Recipes
Quality Dumpling Recipes
Recipes from Ireland
Savory Scottish Recipes
Scandinavian Holiday Recipes
Scandinavian Smorgasbord Recipes

Scandinavian Style Fish and Seafood Recipes
Scandinavian Sweet Treats
Slavic Specialties
Splendid Swedish Recipes
Ukrainian Recipes
License to Cook Arizona Style
License to Cook Iowa Style
License to Cook Kansas Style
License to Cook Minnesota Style
License to Cook New Mexico Style
License to Cook Texas Style
License to Cook Wisconsin Style
Outstanding Oregon Recipes
Waffles, Flapjacks, Pancakes (Scandinavia & Around the World.)

PENFIELD PRESS • 215 BROWN STREET • IOWA CITY, IA 52245-5842

Contents

(contd.)

Contents *(contd.)*

> "A piece of bread in the pocket is better than
> a feather in the hat."
>
> Swedish Proverb: from *Scandinavian Proverbs*

About the Author

Kerstin Olsson came to America from Sweden in 1961 to serve as a nurse at the Pennsylvania Hospital in Philadelphia. She has stayed (she became a naturalized citizen in 1987) as the wife of neurosurgeon John Van Gilder. The Van Gilders are the parents of four children, all raised on traditional Swedish foods. Kerstin owns and manages a kitchen shop with Constance Champion in Iowa City, Iowa. In comparing the foods of her native Sweden to the American diet, Kerstin notes: "We Swedes are fish (herring) and potatoes people. We do not have many meats and the food is lighter than in America. We do not fry as much. We do not have a strong vegetable tradition because of the short growing season. You can have a festive meal of potatoes, herring and aquavit that is fit for a king as well as a peasant. The companionship is the important thing. We don't worry as much when we entertain in Sweden. It's the people that matter."

Swedish-American Cover Child

Sara Sofia Anderson, pictured on the cover, was approximately one- and one-half years old when this picture was taken in the fall of 1993 by her mother. She is the daughter of Charlotte J. and Dean Anderson, who own and operate Anderson Butik in Lindsborg, Kansas. Dean also directs Anderson Scandinavian Tours.

Sara's Swedish folk-style outfit was made for her first *Svensk Hyllningsfest.* The *särk* (white dress) is made of an old, beautifully decorated family sheet. A *"särk"* and an apron are the two basic parts included in almost all Swedish folk costumes. Sara's cap is a so-called *"dala-hätta"* named after the province of Dalarna. Folk costumes for little girls there include similar caps with floral design.

Sara's rolling dala horse was made by local craftsmen from Lindsborg.

Cooking the Naturally Delicious Way

Foods for Swedish meals include: herring, potatoes, marinated salmon, venison, mutton, crayfish, anchovies, parsley, dill, chives, thyme, horseradish, blueberries, lingonberries, cloudberries (the Gold of the North), cream, almonds, apples, gooseberries, currants, salt pork, sour milk, turnips, mushrooms from the forest, and all the other natural foods of the seasons. Kerstin Olsson Van Gilder says, "We also have big parties during the elk, venison and wild rabbit hunting seasons." Midsummer menus feature different kinds of pickled herring and boiled new potatoes with fresh dill and garden-fresh strawberries.

Some of the recipes in this book are from *Delicious Swedish Food* published by Lilla Sällskapet, an organization limited to a membership of 21 Swedish men and

(contd.)

women from a variety of professions who are interested in preserving and promoting Swedish gastronomic traditions. Once a month, they attend dinner meetings where they savor the foods and traditions. The group's recognition of the most authentic traditional Swedish dinner fare found in the restaurants of Stockholm is a highly regarded commendation.

Home fare for Swedish families includes: meatballs, tiny thin pancakes, fried Baltic herring, fried salted herring, pea soup with pork, and beef stew. In Sweden, *ostkaka,* the curd cake "has made its way from farm kitchens to the supermarkets," according to *A Small Treasury of Swedish Food* by the Swedish Dairies' Association and the Swedish Farmers' Meat Marketing Association. It is made from fresh curds and eggs and oven-baked. *Ostkaka* is served with jam or berries and is delicious with whipped cream. Swedish-Americans often have this treat at Christmastime, at church dinners, or at special parties. *(contd.)*

Cooking the Natural Way *(contd.)*

From southern Sweden came the *spettekaka,* a pyramid ring cake baked on a spit. Kerstin Olsson Van Gilder reports that it is so complicated and time-consuming to bake and assemble that most Swedes now buy the cake from bakeries.

The island of Gotland specializes in smoked flatfish, *gotlandsflundror.*

Pepparkakor, the spicy gingerbread cookies, are a must for Christmas. These are exported to America and can be found in tins decorated with the wonderful Carl Larsson paintings.

The Smörgåsbord Accented with Aquavit

The herring is a delicacy and the backbone of the smörgåsbord, according to *Delicious Swedish Food* published by Lilla Sällskapet. The smörgåsbord is served on a long table similar to a buffet; the guests help themselves. A variety of herring dishes begins the incredible offering of wonderful foods—steaming boiled potatoes, thick sour cream, chopped chives and sliced onions. There will be jellied fish, cold cuts of roast beef, meats of wild game, sliced tongue and pâtés, salads and relishes. *Jansson's Temptation* (page 41, this book) is a must. A mini-smörgåsbord may consist of a small plate of butter, cheese, bread and herring. All authentic Swedish smörgåsbords include Swedish aquavit, or schnäpps and a chaser of beer. Kerstin Olsson Van Gilder says, "We also cook with wine and aquavit." Aquavit is a clear liquor made from the potato and finished with a variety of flavors such as anise, caraway, fennel, bitter orange peel and sherry. Aquavit should be enjoyed at a temperature of 34 degrees.

Foods for Special Days and Seasons

Lent: The *semla* or special bun, made from wheat flour, is split and filled with almond paste and whipped cream; served with coffee or in a bowl with hot milk and cinnamon.

Lady Day, the feast day of the Annunciation: Waffles with jam and cream.

Easter: Hard-boiled eggs and egg dishes on the Saturday before Easter. Try eggs and pickled herring.

Walpurgis Night, April 30, welcomes spring with bonfires and songs. Fresh salmon marinated in salt, sugar, pepper and fresh dillweed is a sign of the abundance of the season. The *gravad lax* is served with a special mustard sauce.

(contd.)

Foods for Special Days and Seasons *(contd.)*

Some Swedes prefer smoked fish, cold or heated. Smoked fish is good with fermented cream spiced with one or more finely chopped fresh herbs, chives, dill, parsley or spinach.

Midsummer's Day, end of June: Delicate new potatoes, boiled with dill, seasoned with butter; sweet, pickled herring, fermented cream and chopped chives for lunch. Fresh strawberries for dessert.

Crayfish Season, August 8: Crayfish, bread, butter and cheese.

Autumn: Fresh lamb, fruit, mushrooms, lingonberries and cloudberries.

(contd.)

Foods for Special Days and Seasons *(contd.)*

Winter: Pea soup from dried yellow peas and lightly salted pork, and thin pancakes with jam. Swedish-Americans gather in their churches and halls for traditional Thursday night pea soup dinners. Brown beans, fried pork, potatoes and turnips are used in a variety of dishes.

St. Lucia Day, December 13: This is the first day of the Christmas season that *lussekatter,* saffron flavored bread, is served. In families, the first piece is served by the oldest daughter, who wears on her head a wreath with the lighted candles in it. This festive day heralds the beginning of the holiday season.

Christmas: The saffron-flavored bread is a specialty for Christmas. Celebrations with great foods abound from Christmas Eve to the 20 days after Christmas. Glögg is the beverage of the season.   -13-   *(contd.)*

Foods for Special Days and Seasons *(contd.)*

Christmas Eve dinner includes ham and boiled cabbage. Swedes like shredded red cabbage, sweet and sour. Kale is part of the menu, finely chopped and cooked as spinach. Then there is, of course, the traditional *lutfisk* along with many of the smörgasbord dishes such as herring salad, pickled beetroot, small meatballs, etc. Thick rice pudding with the lucky almond is served with sugar, cinnamon and often a touch of butter. Cold pudding or porridge is mixed with whipped cream and served with fruit syrup or orange sections. Special Christmas treats include tart shells baked in the small fluted baking tins, then filled with jam and topped with whipped cream. Recipes for some of the foods are found in this book:

Glögg

1 bottle red wine
3 to 6 Tbs. schnäpps (or vodka
    or similar spirits)
1 ginger root, whole
2 pieces of stick cinnamon

1/2 tsp. cardamom seeds
6 to 8 cloves
1/3 cup seedless raisins
3 Tbs. blanched almonds

Pour into a saucepan 1 bottle red wine and schnäpps. Add the ginger root, stick cinnamon, cardamom seeds and cloves. Let stand and draw. To serve, heat the cordial almost to a boil. Pour it piping hot over raisins and almonds in small mugs or glasses.

A "Mary" Swede

24 oz. tomato juice, chilled
4 oz. vodka, cold
4 oz. aquavit, cold
1/2 Tbs. Tabasco sauce
1/2 tsp. celery salt

1/4 tsp. ground caraway seed
1 Tbs. (or more) finely chopped
   fresh dill
carrot sticks, celery sticks with leaves,
   cucumber slices and cherry tomatoes

Whisk together first 7 ingredients until well-blended. Chill over 1 hour. Stir and pour into short, 12-oz. glasses and garnish with carrots, celery, tomatoes and cucumbers.

Note: Store the vodka and aquavit in your freezer. The alcohol will prevent freezing, and you'll never have to worry about drinks being too warm.

Michelle Nagle Spencer

Fruit Punch Liquor — Glögg

4 oranges, seeds removed
2 small lemons, seeds removed
1 cup pitted prunes
1 cup raisins
7 to 8 cinnamon sticks

20 cracked cardamom pods
24 whole almonds
20 whole cloves
4 25-oz. bottles California port wine
25 oz. 190-proof grain alcohol or
    110-proof vodka or aquavit

Cut oranges and lemons into eighths. Combine all fruit and spices in a large pan. Cook for 20-30 minutes into a "fruit soup," stirring occasionally. While fruit is cooking, pour wine into a large porcelain pan. Cover and bring to a boil, but do not cook. Pour fruit mixture into wine pan. Cover and bring to a boil again. When mixture begins to boil, pour in the alcohol, cover and bring to a boil again. *(contd.)*

Fruit Punch Liquor (contd.)

Turn off heat. Holding the cover of the pan at rim of pan as a shield, ignite the mixture with a match. Let burn for 30 seconds, and replace cover on pan. Strain fruit mixture for other use. Bottle. Tastes best when served warm.

Editor's note: For a non-alcoholic glögg, the Swedes mix 2 parts black currant juice and 1 part apple juice, and heat with the following seasonings: 1 or 2 cinnamon sticks, cardamom seeds (about a dozen) and dried orange peel. Serve in cups into which almonds and raisins have been added. If black currant juice is not available, try substituting cranberry juice.

Dip in the Kettle

Dopp i Grytan

1 2-lb. chunk beef
1 2-lb. chunk lean pork
1 2-lb. chunk veal (optional)
salt and pepper to taste
1 bay leaf

2 rings potato sausage
1 large onion, cut up
carrots and potatoes, cut in chunks
(amount depends on number to be
served)

A day or two before serving, cook beef, pork and veal in large kettle with water. Add salt, pepper and bay leaf. Cook until tender. Add potato sausage during last 45 minutes of cooking. Let cool thoroughly and skim off all fat. On the morning of the day of serving, cut the meats into serving-sized pieces. Bring the stock and meat to a boil again, adding onion, carrots and potatoes, and slowly simmer until serving time.

(contd.)

Serve from the kettle on the stove with lots of bread, hardtack, cold root beer, and cookies for dessert.

This should serve about 15. For economy, less meat could be used. If more broth is desired, bouillon cubes and hot water could be added.

NOTE: This is a meal served traditionally at noon the day before Christmas.

Gertrude says, "The beauty of this meal is its simplicity and the communion and fellowship it promotes."

Gertrude Lundholm, Rock Island, Illinois
from Superbly Swedish: Recipes and Traditions

Summer Soup

Sommarsoppa

3 small carrots
1 cup small green peas,
    fresh or frozen
3 1/2 oz. fresh spinach
6 to 8 small cauliflower florets
2 cups water

1 1/2 to 2 tsp. salt
2 cups milk
1 Tbs. flour
1 egg yolk
3 Tbs. heavy cream
3 Tbs. finely chopped parsley

Cut vegetables into small pieces, or strips, and cook together in 2 cups salted water. As the spinach needs only 5 minutes, add when the other vegetables are almost done. Take up vegetables with a slotted spoon and keep warm. Heat, but do not boil, milk and vegetable broth together in a pan.

(contd.)

Summer Soup *(contd.)*

Add flour, blended with a little milk. Beat egg yolk and cream. Add to hot liquid along with vegetables and chopped parsley. Warm but do not boil. Serve with cheese sandwiches. Serves 3 to 4.

Note: Depending on what is in season or convenient, any mixture of vegetables can be used—young parsnips, celery, small onions, tender green pea pods, green beans, broccoli, kohlrabi, etc.

Lilla Sällskapet

Swedish Kale Soup   Grönkålssoppa

1 to 1 1/2 lbs. fresh kale or 10 oz.
   frozen chopped kale (thawed)
1 qt. water
1 tsp. salt

2 Tbs. butter
4 Tbs. flour
3 cups chicken bouillon
1/3 cup heavy cream
salt and pepper to taste

If using fresh kale, clean kale leaves and remove the leaves from the stems. Simmer in salted water 4-6 minutes. Drain. Set aside. Melt butter. Add flour and stir in chicken bouillon a little at a time. Simmer for 2-4 minutes. Combine 1 cup of soup and drained kale; blend in blender until kale is very finely chopped. Return to the soup; add salt and pepper to taste. Just before serving, add cream. Serve soup with *frikadeller*. Hard-cooked quartered eggs are served as a garnish. Serves 4 to 6.

Pea Soup with Pork   Ärter med Fläsk

2 cups dried yellow peas
6 cups cold water
1 medium-sized chopped onion

1 tsp. leaf marjoram
1/2 tsp. thyme
3/4 to 1 lb. pork hocks
salt

Soak peas in water overnight, then drain. In a 3-quart pot, cover peas with 6 cups water. Bring to a boil. Skim off any pea husks that rise to surface. Add the chopped onion, marjoram, thyme and pork. Again bring to a boil. Lower heat and simmer with pot covered for about 1 1/2-2 hours. Season with salt. Serve hot soup with a few pieces of pork in each serving bowl.

Ham Rolls

Fyllda Skinkrulader

1 cup cooked green peas	1/2 cup heavy cream, whipped
1 apple, sliced	1/2 cup mayonnaise
1 tsp. lemon juice	1 Tbs. prepared horseradish
2 hard-cooked eggs, chopped	8 slices boiled ham
1 10-oz. pkg. frozen asparagus spears	lettuce

Combine peas, apple, lemon juice and eggs. Chill. Cook asparagus and chill. Whip cream and add mayonnaise and horseradish. Stir dressing into vegetable mixture. Place equal number of asparagus spears on each slice of ham. Top with pea mixture. Roll ham to form logs. Place ham rolls on lettuce to serve.

Kerstin says: "Use for appetizer or a spring luncheon."

Herring Salad   ♦ Sill Salad

2 matjes herring fillets, diced
1 1/2 cups cold boiled potatoes, diced
1 1/2 cups pickled beets, diced
1/3 cup dill pickles, diced
3/4 cup apple, diced
4 to 6 Tbs. liquid from pickled beets

2 Tbs. vinegar
2 Tbs. sugar
lettuce leaves
parsley
hard-cooked egg, sliced

Combine the first 5 ingredients. Mix the beet liquid, vinegar, and sugar together, and stir carefully into the fish mixture. Pack salad into an oil-greased, 5-cup mold. Chill several hours before serving. To serve, unmold onto lettuce leaves and garnish with egg and parsley.

Kerstin says: "Wonderful for a smörgåsbord."

Cold Mustard Sauce   Kall Senaps Sås

2 Tbs. mustard
1 Tbs. sugar
1 Tbs. vinegar

6 Tbs. oil
6 Tbs. sour cream
plenty of finely chopped fresh dill

Mix mustard, sugar, and vinegar in a bowl. Add oil a little at a time until well blended. The sauce will thicken rapidly and must be stirred vigorously. Finally, add the sour cream and plenty of finely chopped dill.

Pickled Herring

Glasmästare Sill

3 to 4 large salted herring
1 cup vinegar
1/2 cup sugar
1 bay leaf, crushed

1 tsp. whole allspice, crushed
1/2 tsp. mustard seeds
10 whole cloves
1 medium-sized red onion, thinly sliced
1 carrot, peeled and thinly sliced

Clean herring and soak in cold water about 12 hours, changing water at least twice. Cut herring diagonally into 1-inch pieces. Boil vinegar and sugar together, then cool. Mix crushed bay leaf, allspice, mustard seeds and whole cloves. In a glass jar, arrange some of the spice mixture, herring pieces, onion and carrot; continue in layers. Pour the cooled vinegar mixture over the layers, cover, and refrigerate at least 12 hours. Serves 6 to 8.

Kerstin says: "Wonderful with boiled potatoes."

Sherry Pickled Herring   Sherry Sill

2 salted herring, filleted and skinned   4 Tbs. vinegar
1 large onion, thinly sliced   1/3 cup water
1/2 cup sherry   1/2 cup sugar
    6 whole allspice, crushed

Soak herring in cold water for 24 hours, changing water at least 3 times. Cut herring diagonally into 1-inch pieces. Arrange herring and onion slices in a jar. Combine the sherry, vinegar, water, sugar, and allspice; pour over herring. Cover jar tightly, and refrigerate at least 24 hours. Serve with boiled potatoes or on a smörgåsbord.

Matjes Herring   Matjes Sill

1 can (7 oz.) matjes herring
1 red onion, sliced in rings
fresh dill sprigs

3/4 cup sour cream
4 Tbs. chopped chives
1 lb. unpeeled potatoes, preferably
   small new ones

Cut herring fillets diagonally into 1-inch pieces. Arrange on serving dish and garnish with fresh dill and onion rings. Serve sour cream and chives either mixed together or in separate dishes. A large bowl of steaming potatoes is placed on the table and each guest peels his own. In Sweden this first course is not complete without rye crisp bread, butter and a strong hard cheese.

Kerstin says: "Matjes herring may be purchased in Scandinavian shops and specialty meat markets."

Lilla Sällskapet

Herring Pudding   # Sill Pudding

2 salted herring
2 medium-sized onions, sliced
1 Tbs. butter or margarine
1 lb. cold boiled potatoes, peeled
    and sliced

3 eggs
3 Tbs. flour
1 1/2 cups milk
1/4 tsp. pepper
2 Tbs. minced parsley

Skin and fillet herring, and cut into 1/2-inch strips. Soak in cold water for 24 hours, changing the water at least once. Sauté onion in butter. Arrange potatoes, herring and onions in layers in a greased 9-inch round baking dish. Combine eggs, flour, milk and pepper. Beat until blended and pour over potatoes. Place baking dish in another container with about 1 inch of water, and bake at 350° for 40-50 minutes, or until custard is set and top is nicely browned. Serve hot; garnished with parsley. Serves 6.

Smoked Herring Gratin   Böcklinglåda

2 leeks, cut into fine strips   1 1/4 cups milk
1 Tbs. butter   1/2 tsp. salt
2 eggs   1/4 tsp. pepper
                                       8 smoked herring, cleaned and filleted

Sauté leeks in butter until soft. Beat together eggs, milk, salt and pepper. In greased baking dish, alternate layers of leeks and herring. Pour the egg mixture over the herring layers. Bake at 400° for about 15-25 minutes, or until batter is set and top is lightly browned. Serves 6.

Crayfish   Kräftor

2 lbs. crayfish, about 25 to 30
2 1/2 qts. water
1/3 cup plus 1 Tbs. coarse salt

1 lump sugar
lots of dill, preferably the crowns

Combine water, dill, salt and sugar in a very large pot. Cover and bring to a boil. Meanwhile check crayfish, making sure that all are alive. Rinse under cold running water. Drop crayfish into briskly boiling dill water and cover at once. Bring to boil again and cook 7 minutes from the time the water starts boiling. Let cool in cooking water. Place in refrigerator overnight, still in water. When ready to serve, pour off cooking water and remove soggy dill. Arrange crayfish attractively on a large platter and garnish with crowns of fresh dill. Serves 3 to 4.

NOTE: You can obtain crayfish from Galveston, Texas, fish markets.

Lilla Sällskapet

Marinated Salmon

Gravlax

2 1/2 to 3 lbs. fresh salmon, center cut,
    cleaned and scaled
1 large bunch of dill

1/4 cup salt
1/4 cup sugar
2 Tbs. crushed pepper

Cut salmon into 2 boneless fillets, leaving the skin on. Rinse salmon and pat dry with paper towels. In a 13x9-inch glass dish, lay 1 fillet skin side down. Spread dill over fillet. Combine the salt, sugar, and pepper. Sprinkle over dill and top with the second fillet, skin side up. Cover with foil and weigh down with another baking dish and a 5 lb. weight or several cans of food. Refrigerate 48-72 hours. Turn salmon every 12 hours and baste with accumulated juices. To serve, remove the fillets from marinade; scrape away the seasonings. Place salmon skin side down, and slice thin, on a diagonal. Remove skin and arrange on a serving dish. *Gravlax* can be frozen for as long as 3 months. *Kerstin says: "Use as main dish for a spring luncheon."*

Smoked Salmon with Creamed Spinach and Poached Egg

Rökt Lax med Spenatstuvning och Förlorade Ägg

1 pint heavy cream
2 10-oz. bags fresh spinach
2 Tbs. butter
salt, pepper and nutmeg to taste

10 eggs
1 Tbs. white vinegar, approximately
10 slices smoked salmon
10 sprigs dill

Simmer cream to reduce by half. Wash spinach and steam in the water that clings to the leaves, 5-7 minutes. Drain thoroughly, pressing to remove moisture, and purée.

(contd.)

Smoked Salmon with Creamed Spinach and Poached Egg *(contd.)*

Return to heat, adding butter and seasonings to taste. Stir in cream. Set aside.

Butter pan so eggs will not stick. Poach eggs in water to cover, with vinegar added. Plunge eggs in cold water to stop cooking. Trim off uneven edges. Set aside. Reheat spinach. On each plate, arrange spinach with a slice of salmon, an egg and a sprig of dill. Makes 10 servings.

Countess Ulla Wachtmeister, Swedish Embassy, Washington, D.C.
from Superbly Swedish: Recipes and Traditions

Mildly Cured Salmon   Lenrimmad Lax

3 lbs. fresh salmon,
     preferably the middle cut

1 cup coarse salt
3 to 4 qts. water

Make a brine; to each quart of water, add 5 tablespoons of coarse salt. Boil until salt has dissolved and then let cool. For this 3-lb. piece, prepare 3 to 4 quarts of brine. Clean, scale and bone fish. Rub fillets with coarse salt. Place in refrigerator overnight. Next day, rinse fish under cold running water. Place salmon in a bowl and pour brine over, making sure the fish is entirely covered. Refrigerate for 48 hours. When ready to serve, remove from brine and pat dry, and cut into paper-thin slices. Mildly cured salmon is served with lemon wedges and creamed potatoes or creamed spinach. Keep the pepper mill close at hand. Serves 8.

NOTE: In Sweden, a small glass of aquavit might accompany this dish, but a chilled dry white wine or beer will also do.

Lilla Sällskapet

Gentlemen's Delight   Gubbröra

4 hard-cooked eggs
8 to 10 Swedish anchovy fillets
    (a 4 1/2-oz. can)

1 onion, preferably red
1 1/2 to 2 Tbs. butter
2 Tbs. finely chopped parsley

Finely chop eggs, anchovies and onion. Do not mix. Melt butter in a heavy skillet and fry onions until golden brown and transparent. Add anchovies. After 1-2 minutes, gently stir in eggs. Warm thoroughly. Sprinkle with parsley. Serve as a first course with hot buttered toast or Swedish rye crisp bread. Also makes a great night snack! Serves 4.

Lilla Sällskapet

Jansson's Temptation   Jansson's Frestelse

6 medium-sized potatoes, peeled and
    cut into 2x1/4-inch strips
2 Tbs. butter
2 medium-sized onions, thinly sliced
1 3 1/2-oz. can Swedish anchovy
    fillets

dash of pepper
2 Tbs. bread crumbs
3 Tbs. butter
3/4 cup cream or half-and-half

Preheat oven to 400°. Keep potato strips in cold water to prevent discoloration. Melt 2 tablespoons butter in skillet and add onions; cook until soft, but not brown, about 5 minutes. Pat potatoes dry. Arrange layers of potatoes, onions and anchovies in a greased 1 1/2- to 2-quart baking dish. Begin and end with potatoes. Dot casserole with butter and sprinkle with pepper and bread crumbs. Pour cream around the casserole. Bake in the center of the oven until the potatoes are tender, and most of the liquid is absorbed, about 45-60 minutes. Serves 4 to 6.

Lutfisk

Lutfisk

whole lutfisk

2 Tbs. butter

Thick cream sauce:
3 Tbs. butter
1 cup cream

3 Tbs. flour
1 1/2 cups milk

Drop lutfisk into salted water and cook 7-10 minutes. Drain; skin and remove all bones. Cut up and place in top of double boiler. Make a thick cream sauce and pour over the fish, not stirring much. Add the 2 tablespoons butter and simmer about a half hour. Serve with mustard sauce.

Jeanne Coppage Honette, Stanton, Iowa
(her mother's recipe)
from Superbly Swedish: Recipes and Traditions

Lutfisk Pudding

Lutfiskpudding

3 lbs. lutfisk
2 1/2 cups cooked rice
1/4 lb. butter, melted
1 1/4 cups cream

5 egg yolks, beaten
5 egg whites, beaten stiff
salt and pepper to taste
bread crumbs

Cook the fish. Flake when cool. Add cooked rice, melted butter, cream and egg yolks. Fold in the egg whites. Season with salt and pepper to taste. Pour into buttered casserole and bake at 350° for 35 minutes. Do not fill casserole to top, as pudding puffs up when baked. Sprinkle with bread crumbs for last 10 minutes of baking.

Esther A. Albrecht, Moline, Illinois
from Superbly Swedish: Recipes and Traditions

Oven-Fried Smelts or Small Herring

Stekt Strömming Utan Matos

1 lb. fish, with heads and tails removed; cleaned and boned but left whole along the backs

salt
3/4 cup chopped dill and parsley
1/2 cup dry bread crumbs
5 to 6 Tbs. butter, melted

Preheat oven to 475°. Rinse fish and pat dry with paper toweling. Sprinkle on both sides with salt. With skin-side out, form sandwiches and fill with dill and parsley mixture. Dip in dry bread crumbs. Put butter in baking dish and place in oven. When dish is hot, remove and arrange fish on bottom. Baste with melted butter. Bake for 8-10 minutes. Turn off oven. Remove and turn fish over. Return to oven for 5 minutes. Of course, you can fry them in a heavy skillet if you prefer. Serve with mashed potatoes. Serves 3 to 4.

VARIATION: Fill fish with table mustard and chopped leeks, or with grated horseradish and parsley.

Lilla Sällskapet

Fillet of Sole with White Sauce, Shrimp and Mushrooms

Rödspätta med Sås, Räkor och Svamp

Fish:
water
white wine
1/2 onion, chopped
1 bay leaf
1 carrot, sliced
4 fillets of sole

Sauce:
2 Tbs. butter
2 Tbs. flour
1/2 cup poaching liquid from fillets
1/2 cup half-and-half
1 small can shrimp
1 small can mushrooms
bread crumbs

(contd.)

Fillet of Sole with White Sauce *(contd.)*

To prepare fish: put enough water in saucepan to cover fish. Add some wine for flavor; add onion, bay leaf and carrot and put pan on medium heat. Add sole and poach. Simmer for 4-5 minutes. Remove sole to serving platter and keep warm. Reserve poaching liquid.

To make sauce: melt butter in saucepan. Add flour, 1/2 cup poaching liquid and half-and-half. Stir in shrimp and mushrooms, and cook until heated through. Pour white sauce over fillets; sprinkle with bread crumbs, and place under broiler for 2-3 minutes before serving. Serves 4.

Notes about Swedish Meatballs

Kerstin says: "There are as many meatball recipes as there are Swedish families and Swedish-American families. All meatball recipes can be made into meat loaves. My husband John says my mother's meatballs are the best he's ever eaten. There is no recipe. She uses only fresh ground pork and then a little sugar, salt, onion and pepper. Cook the same way you would any meatballs. When my mom, Hildur Rasmusson, was young, she got a prize from the Crown Prince Gustav, who became Gustav VI, grandfather of the present king. He awarded the prize. She won the prize for cooking the best crayfish. It was in 1924, and she was about 21."

Swedish Meatballs 1   Svenska Köttbullar

Meatballs:

1 lb. lean hamburger
1/4 cup chopped onion
1 tsp. salt
1/4 tsp. pepper

1/4 tsp. ground allspice
1/4 cup milk
1 egg
3 slices dry bread, crusts removed

Sauce 1:

2 Tbs. fat, drippings from meatballs
2 Tbs. flour

2 cups water or milk or half of each
salt to taste

Sauce 2:

melted butter

To make meatballs: put milk, egg, onion, salt, pepper, allspice, and broken bread into blender and blend at a medium speed for 2 minutes. Combine mixture with meat, and shape into small balls. *(contd.)*

-48-

Swedish Meatballs 1 *(contd.)*

To prepare with Sauce 1: stir together all ingredients for sauce and boil 3 minutes, stirring constantly. Add meatballs and simmer 15-20 minutes. This makes a thin sauce.

To prepare with Sauce 2: brown the meatballs, and simmer until done. Pour melted butter over to serve.

I served my meatballs to an American Indian friend and her two pre-teen daughters. The next thing I heard is that the girls were making them frequently.

Helen Blanck

Swedish Meatballs 2   Svenska Köttbullar

1/3 lb. lean ground beef
1/3 lb. ground pork
1/3 lb. ground veal
1/4 cup chopped onion
1 tsp. salt

1/2 tsp. pepper
1/2 tsp. ground allspice
1/4 cup milk
1 egg
4 slices Swedish rye bread, crusts
    removed

Mix all ingredients except meat in a blender at medium speed for 2 minutes. Add mixture to meat and mix well. Make into small balls; place in an ungreased baking dish, and bake at 325° for 45 minutes. Serve with melted butter, or Sauce 1 (page 48).

Helen Blanck

Swedish Meatballs 3   Svenska Köttbullar

1 Tbs. chopped onion
1 tsp. butter
1/3 cup bread crumbs
2/3 cup water, milk or cream
3/4 lb. ground beef
1/4 lb. ground pork
1/8 tsp. allspice

1/8 tsp. ginger
1/8 tsp. nutmeg
1 1/2 tsp. salt
1/4 tsp. white pepper
1/2 tsp. sugar
butter for frying

Sauté onion in butter. Soak bread crumbs in water, milk or cream. Add remaining ingredients. Shape into small balls. Fry in hot butter. Serves 4 as a main dish.
NOTE: May be frozen in a casserole dish and baked, unthawed, at 350° for 1 hour. Add water or gravy to casserole before freezing.

Mrs. Wendell A. Johnson, Ames, Iowa

Swedish Meatballs 4   Svenska Köttbullar

1 lb. ground beef
1/2 lb. ground pork
1 cup mashed potatoes
1 small onion, grated

2 slices bread soaked in 1/2 cup water
salt and pepper
1 egg
butter or oil for frying

If possible, have butcher grind meats together twice to make meat fine; otherwise, mix meats until well blended. Mix in remaining ingredients. Form into small balls. Fry in butter or oil over medium heat, turning frequently. Reduce heat and simmer, covered. Cook 20-30 minutes total. Add water if necessary. For more flavor, fry a sliced onion with the meatballs.

NOTE: May be made ahead and frozen. Reheat in oven, chafing dish or skillet.

Prof. and Mrs. C. Robert Larson, Wartburg College, Waverly, Iowa
from Superbly Swedish: Recipes and Traditions

Swedish Meatballs 5 Svenska Köttbullar

1 lb. lean ground beef
1 small onion, grated and preferably red
1 tsp. salt
1 to 1 1/2 tsp. ground allspice

1 egg yolk
1/2 cup unsweetened bread, soaked in
   1/2 cup hot water
butter for frying

Combine ground beef, onion, salt, allspice, egg yolk and soaked bread. Mix thoroughly until smooth. Shape one small meatball and fry in butter in heavy skillet to check taste. Correct seasoning with salt and allspice as desired. Shape meatballs. This is easier if you dip your hands into cold water before shaping, or use 2 spoons. Fry meatballs, 8-10 at a time, in melted butter over moderate heat. By shaking skillet now and then, the meatballs will retain their round form and will brown evenly on all sides. Serve with mashed potatoes and lingonberry or cranberry preserves. Serves 4 to 6.

Lilla Sällskapet

Swedish Meatballs 6   Svenska Köttbullar

Meatballs:
1 lb. ground beef
1 lb. ground pork
4 Tbs. finely chopped onion
1 tsp. butter
1 egg
1 Tbs. sugar

1 1/2 tsp. salt
1/2 tsp. pepper
3 Tbs. dry bread crumbs
4 Tbs. beer
1 large boiled potato, mashed
2 Tbs. butter

Gravy:
drippings from meatballs
1 Tbs. flour
3/4 cup half-and-half

1/4 cup water
salt to taste

(contd.)

Swedish Meatballs 6 *(contd.)*

Meatballs: Grind meats together twice. Sauté onion in 1 teaspoon of the butter. Let cool. Mix all ingredients, except butter. Shape mixture into small balls about 1 inch in diameter. In a heavy 10- to 12-inch skillet, melt 2 tablespoons butter over high heat. Reduce heat and brown balls on all sides, then cook 8-10 minutes, or until there is no trace of pink meat inside. Serve as hors d´oeuvres.

Gravy: If meatballs are to be served as a main course, remove from skillet; add flour to drippings, and stir until smooth. Add half-and-half, water, and salt to taste. Boil 2-3 minutes, stirring constantly until thick and smooth. Pour over meatballs and serve.

Christina's Meatballs 7

Meatballs:
2 lbs. ground beef
1/2 cup oatmeal
1 egg

1 Tbs. dried onion flakes
dash Worcestershire sauce
1/2 tsp. nutmeg
4 cups cooked rice

Gravy:
1 Tbs. flour

1/2 cup beer
dash nutmeg

To make meatballs: combine all ingredients, except cooked rice, and mix well. Shape into balls and brown in a skillet. Remove meatballs from pan.

To make gravy: add flour to the meatball drippings; stir until smooth, and add beer and nutmeg. If too thick, add more beer. If too thin, add more flour. Stir meatballs into the gravy. Serve over steaming hot rice.

Mrs. Dora Benander Koch

Swedish Meatballs 8   Svenska Köttbullar

1 lb. ground beef
1 lb. ground pork
1 lb. ground veal
1 onion, chopped fine
margarine

1 cup milk
1 1/2 tsp. salt
1/2 tsp. pepper
2/3 cup bread crumbs
bouillon, about 1/3 cup

Grind the three meats together twice. Sauté onion in margarine and let cool. Mix all ingredients, except bouillon, together well. Shape into small balls and brown. Place in a covered casserole with bouillon and simmer in 350° oven for 45-60 minutes.

Swedish Meatballs 9   Svenska Köttbullar

Meatballs:
1 1/2 lbs. lean ground beef
1/2 cup chopped onion
3/4 cup dry bread crumbs
1 Tbs. dry parsley
1 1/2 tsp. salt

1/8 tsp. pepper
1 tsp. Worcestershire sauce
1 egg, slightly beaten
1/2 cup milk
3 Tbs. shortening

Sauce:
1/4 cup flour
1 tsp. paprika
1 Tbs. salt

1/8 tsp. pepper
2 cups water
3/4 cup sour cream

To make meatballs: mix all ingredients, except shortening, together and form into small balls about the size of walnuts.

(contd.)

Swedish Meatballs 9 *(contd.)*

In a heavy skillet, brown meatballs in shortening. Turn frequently to brown on all sides. Place browned meatballs in baking dish and cover with sauce. Simmer in oven at 300° for 30 minutes. Makes about 50 meatballs.

To make sauce: cook flour, paprika, salt, pepper and water until thickened, stirring often. Reduce heat; add sour cream, and stir until smooth. Do not boil.

NOTE: Can be frozen with or without sauce.

Swedish Meatballs 10   Svenska Köttbullar

1 cup fresh bread crumbs
1 1/2 cups milk, divided
1 lb. ground beef
1 to 2 tsp. salt
1/2 tsp. pepper

2 Tbs. finely chopped onion
1 egg, beaten
3 Tbs. butter or margarine
1 Tbs. flour

Combine bread crumbs with 3/4 cup milk and set aside for 10 minutes. Add beef, salt, pepper, onion and egg; mix together. Shape into 1-inch balls. Melt butter in large skillet and brown meatballs on all sides. Remove meatballs from skillet and keep in warm place. Pour fat from pan, reserving 1 tablespoon. Blend flour in reserved fat and gradually stir in remaining milk. Cook over medium heat, stirring constantly, until thickened and smooth. Pour over meatballs and serve with lingonberry preserves. Makes 4 servings.

Hamburger à la Lindström

Biff à la Lindström

1 lb. lean ground beef
2 egg yolks
1/2 cup liquid from pickled beets
1/3 cup whipping cream
2 tsp. salt
pepper to taste

4 Tbs. finely chopped onion, sautéed
   in butter (or to taste)
2 to 4 Tbs. drained, finely chopped
   capers
1/2 cup drained, finely chopped pickled
   beets
butter for frying

In a large bowl mix well the ground beef, egg yolks, juice from pickled beets, whipping cream, salt and pepper.

(contd.)

Hamburger à la Lindström   *(contd.)*

Gently stir in sautéed onions, capers and pickled beets. Shape into patties about 2 1/2-3 inches in diameter. Melt butter in large heavy skillet over moderate heat and fry patties 3-4 minutes on a side. They should be rosy inside.

VARIATIONS: Swedes often serve these hamburgers with a fried egg on top of each patty. Or you can cut small rounds of toast and spread a thick layer of meat mixture completely covering toast. Fry, meat side down, for 2 -3 minutes. Place on buttered ovenproof plate, toast side down. Bake at 400° for 5 -6 minutes and serve immediately.

Mrs. Lambert Dahlsten, Lindsborg, Kansas
from Superbly Swedish: Recipes and Traditions

Swedish Boiled Beef   Pepparrotskött

3 lbs. beef chuck with bone
1 qt. water
1 1/2 tsp. salt
1 onion, peeled and quartered
Gravy:
1 cup cooking liquid, strained
1 cup half-and-half

1 yellow turnip, peeled and diced
1 carrot, peeled and sliced
2 stalks celery, sliced
6 to 10 whole black peppercorns

2 Tbs. flour
3 to 4 Tbs. prepared horseradish

Cover meat with water in a heavy saucepan. Add salt and onion. Bring to a boil. Simmer, then skim. Add remainder of vegetables and peppercorns. Simmer until meat is tender, about 1 more hour. Remove meat and vegetables and keep warm. **To make gravy:** bring 1 cup strained liquid and the half-and-half to a boil. Add flour mixed with 1/4 cup water, stir and boil for 2 minutes. Add horseradish to gravy. Serves 4 to 6.

Swedish Pot Roast   Slott Stek

3 1/2 to 4 lbs. beef rump roast
1 tsp. salt
1/2 tsp. pepper
2 Tbs. margarine
1 1/2 cups beef bouillon
1 bay leaf
1 onion, cut in half

8 whole allspice
6 white peppercorns
1 Tbs. syrup
2 Tbs. vinegar
6 Swedish anchovy fillets
2 Tbs. flour
1/2 cup cream

Rub roast with salt and pepper. In a heavy saucepan, heat margarine, and brown roast well on all sides. Add bouillon, bay leaf, onion, allspice, peppercorns, syrup and vinegar. Place the anchovies on top of the meat. Cover and simmer for about 2 hours or until meat is tender. When meat is ready, add anchovies to juice. Strain juice. Stir in 2 tablespoons flour and 1/2 cup cream to make gravy. Serve with sliced beef.

Sailor's Beef Casserole   Sjömans Biff

1 1/2 lbs. chuck or round of beef
6 medium-sized raw potatoes
3 Tbs. butter
2 large onions, sliced
1 1/2 tsp. salt

pepper
1 1/2 cups hot water
1/2 cup beer
1/4 cup chopped parsley

Cut meat into 1/4-inch slices and pound. Peel potatoes and cut into thick slices. Heat butter; sauté onion and brown meat in it. Layer potatoes, meat and onion in casserole; sprinkle salt and pepper between layers, ending with potatoes. Pour water into frying pan; stir and add this liquid to casserole. Add beer. Cover and bake at 375° for 1-1 1/2 hours or until meat is tender. Sprinkle with chopped parsley. Makes 4 servings. Good served with pickled beets.

The Vasa Restaurant, Lindsborg, Kansas

Sailor's Stew   Sjömans Biff

2 to 3 onions, sliced
2 Tbs. margarine
1 1/2 lbs. round steak, cut into
    8 to 10 portions
2 Tbs. flour

1 tsp. salt
1/2 tsp. pepper
6 to 8 medium-sized potatoes,
    peeled and sliced
1 1/2 cups bouillon

Brown onion in margarine in a heavy skillet; set onion aside when transparent. Coat meat with flour, salt and pepper. Brown meat in hot skillet. In casserole dish place alternate layers of beef, onions and potatoes. Pour bouillon and pan drippings over layers. Cover and simmer in oven at 350° for 1 1/2 hours or until tender. This recipe may also be cooked on top of the stove in a heavy saucepan.

Swedish Stew

Kalops

1/2 tsp. salt	2 onions, peeled and thinly sliced
1/4 tsp. pepper	3 cups water
3 Tbs. flour	2 beef bouillon cubes
3 lbs. beef for stew	10 whole peppercorns
2 Tbs. butter or margarine	2 bay leaves

Mix salt, pepper and flour. Dredge meat with flour mixture. Melt butter or margarine in Dutch oven. Add meat and onion. Brown meat on all sides. Add water, bouillon cubes, peppercorns and bay leaves. Cover and let simmer, stirring occasionally, until meat is tender, about 1 1/2-2 hours. Serves 6.

Kerstin says: "This is a great dish for the pressure cooker."

Old-fashioned Spiced Ham

Cajsa Wargs Kryddskinka

7 to 9 lbs. cured and lightly smoked
    or just lightly smoked ham
2 tśp. whole cloves
2 tsp. whole allspice

2 tsp. rosemary or basil
3 bay leaves
2 tsp. marjoram (or oregano)

Preheat oven to 300°. Remove rind and most of the fat from the ham, and place on a piece of aluminum foil, large enough to wrap entire ham. Place spices in a mortar and crush well. Rub ham on all sides with spice mixture. Wrap ham in foil and seal tightly. Insert a meat thermometer into the thickest part of the ham. Place in oven and bake until the thermometer reads 170°, about 5 hours. Serves 12 to 15.

Lilla Sällskapet

Ham

Prepare ham:
1 10- to 12-lb. ham
1 cup salt
1/4 cup sugar
1/2 Tbs. saltpeter

Brine:
To every quart of water, add:
1/2 cup salt
1 Tbs. sugar
1/4 Tbs. saltpeter

To cook:
water
1 to 2 bay leaves
10 white peppercorns
allspice

Coating:
1 egg white
1 Tbs. prepared mustard or
    dry mustard
2 to 3 tsp. sugar
bread crumbs

(contd.)

Ham *(contd.)*

Wipe ham and rub with mixture of 1 cup salt, 1/4 cup sugar and 1/2 tablespoon saltpeter. Place in a clean wooden or stone crock and refrigerate 1 to 3 days, turning occasionally. Make brine of boiling water, salt, sugar and saltpeter. Cool and pour over ham to cover; weigh down with plate or other heavy object and refrigerate for 10 days. Remove ham, wipe well and place fat side up in boiling water to cover. Return water to boil; add bay leaves, peppercorns and allspice. Simmer until done, about 3 hours. When cooked, skin ham and wipe to remove all loose fat. Return to liquid to cool. Brush with mixture of beaten egg white, mustard and 2 to 3 teaspoons sugar, then sprinkle with bread crumbs. Bake or broil until nicely browned. Strain liquid and season. Ham is ready to serve and liquid can be heated and served as "dip in the pot (or kettle)."

Kerstin says: "As a Swede, you can never get enough ham."

Ragnhild Holm, member
American Swedish Historical Museum, Philadelphia, Pennsylvania
from Superbly Swedish: Recipes and Tradittions

Lamb or Veal in Dill Sauce   Dillkött

Meat:

2 to 2 1/2 lbs. breast, leg or shoulder
    of lamb, or veal
1 tsp. salt
8 white peppercorns
1 yellow onion

1 leek
2 carrots
1/2 celery root
1 bunch fresh dill sprigs
    or 1 Tbs. dried dill

Sauce:

2 Tbs. butter
2 Tbs. flour
2 cups stock
1 Tbs. white vinegar
1/2 tsp. lemon juice

2 tsp. sugar
1/2 cup heavy cream
2 egg yolks
3 to 4 Tbs. finely chopped dill
    or 1 Tbs. dried dill

(contd.)

Lamb or Veal in Dill Sauce *(contd.)*

For meat: Cut meat into small cubes and place in heat-resistant casserole. Add salt, peppercorns and enough water to cover meat. Bring to boil and skim the surface. Dice vegetables; add with dill to meat. Cover and simmer slowly for 1 1/2 hours or until meat is very tender. Strain and boil stock down to 2 cups.

For sauce: Melt butter in pan and dust flour over, mixing well. Blend in stock, and let sauce boil for 3-5 minutes, stirring often. Add vinegar, lemon juice and sugar. In an enameled or stainless steel pan, cook egg yolks and cream over low heat until thickened. Do not boil. Remove from heat; blend into sauce, season to taste, and add dill. The sourness/sweetness can be adjusted to taste by increasing or decreasing the amounts of vinegar and sugar. Pour sauce over meat or serve separately along with buttered boiled potatoes, or rice and peas. Serves 4.

Lilla Sällskapet

Jellied Meat   Sylta

1 veal shank, cut
2 lbs. lean pork butt
1 Tbs. salt

1 Tbs. whole allspice
4 bay leaves
crushed allspice

Place first 5 ingredients in a pot with enough water to just cover meat. Let boil slowly until about 1 inch of liquid remains in pot. Remove meat and set aside to cool. Remove liquid from heat. Cut meat into bite-sized pieces. Put half of meat in a pan. Sprinkle with 1/2 teaspoon crushed allspice. Top with remainder of meat and more crushed allspice. Bring liquid to a boil and strain onto meat. Press meat down by placing board on it and weighing it down with large stone or other heavy object. Chill well and slice to serve.

Mrs. Wesley (Eileen) Scott, Minneapolis, Minnesota
from Superbly Swedish: Recipes and Traditions

Swedish Loin of Pork   Fläskkarré

15 prunes, pitted
1 3/4 cups water, divided
3 lbs. loin of pork

1 tsp. salt
1/4 tsp. pepper
2 Tbs. flour
cream, optional

Cover prunes with 1 1/2 cups water, bring to a boil. Turn heat off and let cool. Reserve liquid. With a sharp knife make slits the length of the pork loin. Rub roast with salt and pepper and insert cooked prunes in the slits. Place meat in roasting pan; add 1/4 cup water and roast at 350° for 1 1/2-1 3/4 hours. Remove meat when done. Stir flour in drippings and slowly add water and prune liquid. Stir over low heat until thickened and smooth. Add a little cream for a richer tasting gravy. Slice meat and serve with gravy. Serves 4 to 6.

Swedish Veal Rollettes   Kalvkyckling

8 slices ham, 6x4x1/8 inch
8 thin veal cutlets, 1/8 inch thick
3 Tbs. butter

1/2 cup dry white wine
1 cup shredded Swiss cheese

Place ham on veal cutlets. Roll up and hold in place with toothpicks. Melt butter in heavy skillet over medium heat. Brown veal rollettes evenly. Add wine. Cover and simmer on low heat for 7-10 minutes or until meat is tender. Remove rollettes and keep warm. Add cheese to skillet and cook over low heat, stirring constantly, until cheese is melted in wine sauce. Serve sauce over veal rollettes. Serves 8.

Vealburger à la Wallenberg

Wallenbergare

1 lb. lean ground veal, well-chilled
1 tsp. salt
1/2 tsp. white pepper
4 egg yolks

1 to 1 1/4 cups heavy cream
2 Tbs. day-old, crust-free white bread,
    passed through a sieve
butter for frying

Put meat in mixing bowl and season with salt and pepper. Stir in egg yolks, one at a time. Gradually blend in well-chilled cream. Shape patties a good 1/2 inch thick and about 2 1/2 inches in diameter. Sprinkle bread crumbs on both sides of the patties. Fry in butter over low heat, brown on both sides. Serves 4 to 6.

NOTE: In Sweden, these vealburgers are traditionally served with mashed potatoes, tiny green peas and lingonberry or cranberry preserves.

Lilla Sällskapet

Swedish Hash   Pytt Ipanna

1 large onion, chopped
2 Tbs. butter or margarine
2 cups diced beef or pork, cooked

4 to 6 medium-sized potatoes, cooked,
    peeled and diced
salt and pepper to taste
1 Tbs. chopped parsley

In a large heavy skillet, sauté onion in butter or margarine. Add meat, diced potatoes, salt and pepper. Cook until mixture is lightly browned. Sprinkle with parsley. Serve with fried egg and pickled beets. Makes 4 to 6 servings.

Swedish Meat Dumplings   *Frikadeller*

2 Tbs. fine dry bread crumbs
1/3 cup half-and-half
1/2 lb. ground beef
1/2 lb. ground pork
1/2 lb. ground veal

1 egg
3/4 tsp. salt
1/4 tsp. pepper
1 to 2 bouillon cubes
1 qt. water

Soak bread crumbs in half-and-half. Combine beef, pork, veal, egg, salt and pepper. Add crumb mixture and mix well. Shape into small meatballs. In large saucepan, boil water; add 1-2 bouillon cubes. Add meatballs a few at a time and simmer over moderate heat about 5 minutes. Remove with slotted spoon. Drain on paper towels. Keep warm. Serve with dill sauce or lemon sauce. *Frikadeller* are also served in *Grönkålssoppa* (page 25). Serves 6.

Stuffed Cabbage Leaves   Kåldolmar

2 lbs. ground beef
1 lb. pork sausage (not too fat)
2/3 cup rice (or enough for 2 cups cooked)
1 good-sized head of cabbage
1 tsp. cloves

2 tsp. cinnamon
salt to taste (not too much if sausage is heavily seasoned)
1 can golden mushroom soup
flour or cornstarch

Cook rice to make 2 cups to put in the meat mixture (more than 2 cups won't make any difference—it just makes more). Cut the core out of the cabbage. Place in a large pot that has a lid and steam until the leaves look clear. (Don't overcook.) Start cooking the cabbage with the top of the head up, then switch the top down so the thickest part of the head gets a little more steaming. Remove the cabbage to a large platter. Pull the leaves apart and let cool.

(contd.)

Stuffed Cabbage Leaves (contd.)

Stir and mix the cooked rice, meats and spices together and make into thick round patties. Roll in cabbage leaves with the cabbage edges underneath. Place in a small, flat roaster that will hold 12 to 15 *kåldomar*. (Any leftover cabbage leaves can be laid on top and baked with the *kåldomar*.) Add some liquid to the roaster and cover with a lid or foil. Bake at 350° for an hour or more, until the tops are brown. Check occasionally during baking and baste if the leaves are drying out. When done, remove the *kåldomar* and thicken the juice with flour or cornstarch, and add the can of soup. Mix the soup well with the juices; pour over the *kåldomar;* simmer to heat and serve. *Kåldomar* reheat well and can also be frozen.

Ruby Heusinkveld

Swedish Spring Chicken   Vårkyckling

1 whole spring chicken
   (2 1/2 to 3 1/2 lbs.)
1 bunch fresh parsley without stems
1/4 lb. plus 1 tsp. butter

1 Tbs. sugar
salt and pepper to taste
1 cup chicken bouillon
flour
half-and-half

Mix parsley with 1/4 pound softened butter. Reserve 1 tablespoon of this mixture and rub the rest inside the chicken cavity. Rub the reserved butter/parsley, sugar, salt and pepper on outside of chicken. Brown the whole chicken in another teaspoon butter over medium heat, taking about 30 minutes and rotating the chicken to brown on all sides. Add the bouillon to browned chicken, cover and simmer slowly about 45 minutes. Thicken remaining juices with flour and half-and-half. The cook must determine the quantity of flour and half-and-half, depending on the quantity of juice from the chicken. Season to taste. Serve this gravy with the chicken.

Roast Goose

Stekt Gås

1 10- to 12-lb. goose
1/2 lemon
1 tsp. salt

1/4 tsp. black pepper
8 apples, cored and quartered
30 pitted prunes

Wash and dry the goose. Remove fatty portion inside the cavity. Rub the cavity with lemon, salt and pepper. Fill the cavity with the apples and prunes. Close the goose with skewers. Bake in a shallow roasting pan on a rack for 4 1/2 hours at 325°. Check that the juices are yellow and not pink when you pierce the goose.

Serve the goose with potatoes and parsley. Use the apples and prunes as decorations as well as for serving with the goose. The apples and prunes absorb the fat from the goose.

Potato Dumplings   Kroppkakor

7 lbs. potatoes
2 lbs. lean salt pork
1 onion, chopped
6 or 7 eggs

salt to taste
6 to 7 cups flour (enough to make
       dumplings easy to handle)

Boil the potatoes in their jackets. Cool and rice them. Dice or coarsely grind the salt pork. Fry, and when nearly finished, add onion. Set aside to cool. Beat eggs and mix together with riced potatoes, salt to taste, and flour. Shape into cakes about 2 inches in diameter and 1 inch thick. With spoon or knife, insert a teaspoonful of pork mixture into middle of each cake. Boil in salted water about 10 minutes. They will rise to the top. They also may be cut in half and fried. Dumplings may be eaten hot or cold. *This dish is typical of southern Sweden.*

Mrs. Conrad A. Peterson, St. Peter, Minnesota
from Superbly Swedish: Recipes and Traditions

Open Omelet   Äggakaka

5 eggs   scant 1/2 cup flour
1 2/3 cups milk, divided   1/2 tsp. salt

Beat the eggs and a little milk. Add flour and continue to beat until smooth. Add the remainder of the milk and the salt. Heat a little butter in a frying pan; pour in the batter, and cook on moderate heat. While cooking, lift the batter with a fork so that it sets evenly. Turn out the omelet to a plate and slide it back into the frying pan to cook the other side.

VARIATIONS: For a bacon omelet, top with bacon, fried crisp; for a spinach omelet, reduce the milk to 1 1/4 cups and add 1 package thawed chopped spinach (about 6 ounces).

Baked Pancake   Ugns Pannkaka

2 eggs
2 1/2 cups milk, divided
1/2 tsp. salt

2 tsp. sugar
1 1/2 cups sifted flour

Beat eggs and 1 cup of milk until well blended. Add salt, sugar and flour to make a smooth batter. Stir in the remainder of milk; blend until batter is smooth. Let sit for 10-15 minutes. Butter a 12x8x2-inch baking dish or a 10-inch cast iron skillet. Stir batter and pour into pan. Preheat oven to 400° and bake for 30 minutes, or until pancake is brown and puffy. Serve at once with jam or fresh fruit. Serves 6.

Kerstin says: "This can be used as a main dish and as a dessert. If choosing it for a light lunch dish, brown bacon until crisp; add to batter and bake as above."

Basic Recipe for Pancakes   Pannkako

1 cup milk, divided
2 eggs
3 egg yolks

1/2 cup all-purpose flour
1/2 cup heavy cream
1/2 tsp. salt
2 Tbs. melted butter

Beat eggs and egg yolks with 1/2 cup milk. Sift in flour and beat until smooth. Beat in remaining milk, cream, salt and melted butter. Let batter stand for at least 1 hour. In a lightly greased and well-heated, but not too hot, 6-inch crêpe pan drop 1 1/2-2 tablespoons of batter. These crêpes are to be thin and are browned on one side only. Stir batter now and then. It is not necessary to grease the pan after the first time. Stack the crêpes between layers of paper toweling. Crêpes may be stored in the freezer. Makes about 20 crêpes.

NOTE: This batter recipe is used for filled crêpes and pancakes.

Lilla Sällskapet

Swedish Pancake   Fläskpannkaka

1 cup sifted flour   4 eggs
1 tsp. sugar   2 cups milk
1 tsp. salt   1/2 lb. Canadian bacon or ham

Sift flour into bowl; add sugar and salt. Mix eggs and milk together and then add slowly to dry mixture. Stir until well blended and refrigerate 8 hours. Cube and fry bacon or ham. Beat batter, pour over meat and bake at 400° for 30 minutes or until set and nicely browned. This dish rises up like a soufflé. Serve immediately with lingonberries, syrup, sugar, or topping of your choice. Serves 4.

NOTE: Four individual baking dishes are an excellent way to bake Flaskpannkaka. Also, corn or Mexicorn added to the batter, instead of meat, makes an interesting side dish.

An old Swedish recipe popular with Minnesotans of Swedish descent.
William A. McGonagle

Lacy Potato Pancakes   Rårakor

6 medium-sized baking potatoes
3 eggs
2 Tbs. flour
1 tsp. salt

1/4 tsp. black pepper
2 to 4 Tbs. butter for frying
2 to 4 Tbs. oil for frying

Peel and coarsely grate potatoes. Add eggs, flour, salt and pepper. Heat butter and oil in large skillet over high heat until foam subsides. Use 2 tablespoons of potato mixture for each pancake, flattening them to 3 inches in diameter. Fry 2-3 minutes on each side or until they are golden and crisp. Add more oil and butter after each batch if necessary. Serves 4.

Cabbage Pudding   Kålpudding

1 head cabbage (1 1/2 to 2 lbs.)   1/4 tsp. pepper
1 lb. ground beef   1 egg
1 lb. ground pork   1/3 cup mashed potatoes
3/4 tsp. salt

Remove core and chop cabbage into large pieces. Cook cabbage in boiling water until it wilts. Drain. Combine beef, pork, salt, pepper, egg and mashed potatoes. Work mixture until well mixed. In a well-greased 2-quart casserole dish, alternate layers of meat mixture and cabbage, the last layer being meat. Cover casserole and place in large baking pan with 1 inch of boiling water, and bake for 1-1 1/2 hours at 400°. Let stand 5 minutes, then turn out onto warm serving platter. Serves 6.

Creamed Potatoes

Stuvad Potatis

10 medium-sized (1 1/2 lbs.) potatoes
2 Tbs. butter
1 1/2 cups part milk, part cream

1 1/2 tsp. salt
1/3 cup finely chopped dill, parsley,
    chives or leeks– any one
    or a mixture

Peel the potatoes and dice into small cubes. Melt butter in a pan and briefly sauté the potatoes. Pour milk/cream over potatoes and add salt. Cover and cook over low heat until the potatoes are soft, about 15-20 minutes. Add finely chopped dill, parsley, chives or leeks. Serve with smoked meat or fish, with ham or tongue, or with lightly cured salmon. Serves 3 to 4.

VARIATION: In southern Sweden, finely chopped yellow onions are sautéed together with the raw potatoes.

Lilla Sällskapet

Hasselback Potatoes   Hasselback Potatis

12 medium-sized (2 lbs.) potatoes
3 Tbs. melted butter, divided
1 to 1 1/2 tsp. salt

1 Tbs. dry bread crumbs
4 Tbs. grated cheese

Preheat oven to 425°. Place peeled potatoes on a flat surface and make 1/8-inch wide vertical slices about 2/3 of the way through the potatoes. It is important that the slices are still joined at the base. Pat dry. With the cut side up, place potatoes in a well-buttered baking dish. Pour 1 1/2 tablespoons melted butter over potatoes and sprinkle liberally with salt. Bake for 30 minutes. Baste with butter every now and then. After 30 minutes, sprinkle with bread crumbs and grated cheese. Return to oven for another 15 minutes, or until the potatoes feel soft when tested with a toothpick. Serves 4 to 6.

Lilla Sällskapet

Mashed Turnips   Rotmos

3/4 lb. yellow turnips, peeled
    and cut into small cubes
1 lb. potatoes, peeled and cut
    into small cubes

1 1/2 cups bouillon or milk
2 Tbs. butter or margarine
1/2 tsp. salt
1/2 tsp. pepper

Boil turnips 15-20 minutes. Add potatoes and boil until tender. Drain and mash vegetables well, adding enough bouillon or milk for desired consistency. Add butter, salt and pepper. Serve with sausage. Serves 4.

Rye Bread   Rågbröd

2 medium potatoes
1 qt. lukewarm potato water
   (reserved from boiling potatoes)
1 Tbs. salt
1/2 cup white sugar
2 pkgs. active dry yeast
4 cups sifted rye flour

1/2 cup sorghum or dark corn syrup
2 eggs
1 1/4 cups brown sugar
1 cup margarine
2 Tbs. crushed fennel seeds
2 Tbs. crushed anise seeds
10 cups white flour, divided

Boil potatoes until soft, mash and add to potato water. Strain, leaving enough liquid to make one quart potato water. Add salt, white sugar and yeast to lukewarm potato water and stir. Let stand 10 to 15 minutes. Add rye flour and beat. Let rise in warm place for 1/2 hour.

(contd.)

Rye Bread *(contd.)*

Mix in sorghum or syrup, eggs, brown sugar, margarine and crushed seeds and beat with egg beater. Add 5 cups of the white flour and continue beating. Turn out on board and knead in the remaining white flour. Knead well for 10 minutes. Let rise in well-greased bowl in warm place until doubled. Form into 6 small round loaves or 6 loaves to fit one-pound-sized pans. Bake at 400° for 10 minutes, then at 325° for 40 minutes.

Jenny Johnson, American Swedish Institute, Minneapolis, Minnesota
from Superbly Swedish: Recipes and Traditions

Swedish Hardtack   # Knäckebröd

1 pt. buttermilk
1/2 cup sugar
1/2 cup butter, melted

1 tsp. salt
7/8 tsp. baking soda
2 cups coarse rye flour
(or enough to form a thick dough)

Mix ingredients to make a thick dough and form into balls (1 inch or so in diameter). Roll the balls in additional flour, then roll very thin with a peg rolling pin. An ordinary rolling pin may be used, but the dough must be scored and pricked before baking. Bake on a cookie sheet at 425° until lightly browned. These wafers are delicious with soup, salad, or cheese.

Elizabeth (Mrs. Einar) Jaderborg, Lindsborg, Kansas
from Superbly Swedish: Recipes and Traditions

Swedish Pastry   Gifflar

Pastry dough:
1 egg
3 Tbs. sugar
1/4 tsp. salt
1/2 tsp. almond extract (optional)
1 cup warm milk
Glaze 1:
1 egg, beaten
Glaze 2:
1 cup confectioners' sugar
2 Tbs. water
1/4 tsp. almond extract

1 cake yeast or 1 pkg. dry yeast
2 1/2 cups flour
1/4 lb. soft-spread margarine
flour for rolling out

(contd.)

Swedish Pastry *(contd.)*

To make pastry dough: beat egg with sugar, salt and almond extract. Stir yeast into warm milk. Let yeast come to the top of milk, then add egg mixture. Add flour. Mix and beat to a shiny dough. (I usually knead it too.) Roll dough into a rectangle 1/4 inch thick. Spread margarine over top. Fold over 1/3 of the long side, then 1/3 of the other long side. Do the same with the short sides. Put this folded pastry in the refrigerator to rest for about 15 minutes. It will rise slightly. Take it out and roll it out as before, spreading with margarine and folding. Let it rest in the refrigerator again and repeat the process one more time. This makes the buns flaky when baked. Finally roll out to 1/2 inch thickness; cut into triangles. Roll triangles from the long side, tucking the pointed end under. Place on baking sheet and let rise until double. Bake at 375° for about 10 minutes or until light brown. Makes about 15.

(contd.)

Swedish Pastry *(contd.)*

For glazing: Either brush on the beaten egg before baking or brush on the confectioners' sugar/water/almond extract mixture after baking. If you freeze some of the rolls, put the sugar glazing on just before serving.

NOTE: These look like dinner rolls, but are lighter and fluffier. They are not as sweet as American coffee bread. They are good with strong Swedish coffee.

Lilly Setterdahl of the Swenson Swedish Immigration Research Center,
Augustana College , Rock Island, Illinois
from Superbly Swedish: Recipes and Tradtions

Christmas Bread   Julbröd

1 pkg. active dry yeast
1/4 cup warm water (105-115°)
3/4 cup lukewarm milk,
    scalded then cooled
1/4 cup sugar
1/4 cup margarine, softened
1 egg
1/2 tsp. ground cardamom
1/2 tsp. salt

1/2 cup raisins
1/2 cup chopped dried mixed fruit
1/4 cup slivered almonds
3 1/4 to 3 1/2 cups flour, divided
1 cup powdered sugar
1 to 2 Tbs. milk
maraschino cherries
walnuts

In large bowl dissolve yeast in warm water. Stir in milk, sugar, margarine, egg, cardamom, salt, raisins, mixed fruit, almonds and 2 cups of flour.

(contd.)

Christmas Bread *(contd.)*

Beat until smooth. Stir in enough of remaining flour to make dough easy to handle. Turn dough onto lightly floured surface; knead until smooth and elastic. Place in greased bowl, cover and let rise until double. Punch down dough. Roll into a 15x9-inch rectangle on lightly floured surface. Roll up tightly lengthwise. Pinch edge of dough into roll to seal well. With sealed edge down, shape into a ring in a lightly greased pie pan. Pinch the ends together. Let rise until double. Bake for 25-30 minutes at 350°.

Make glaze by mixing powdered sugar and 1 to 2 tablespoons milk until smooth. Spread ring with glaze, and garnish with maraschino cherries and nuts.

Gustavus Adolphus College Food Service, St. Peter, Minnesota
from Superbly Swedish: Recipes and Traditions

St. Lucia Buns   Lussekatter

2 pkgs. active dry yeast
1/2 cup warm water (105-115°)
2/3 cup lukewarm milk
   (scalded, then cooled)
1/2 cup sugar
1/2 cup margarine, softened
2 eggs
1/2 tsp. ground cardamom

1 tsp. salt
1/2 tsp. powdered saffron
5 to 5 1/2 cups flour, divided
1/2 cup raisins
margarine, softened
1 egg, slightly beaten
1 Tbs. water
2 Tbs. sugar

Dissolve yeast in warm water. Stir in milk, 1/2 cup sugar, 1/2 cup margarine, 2 eggs, cardamom, salt, saffron and 3 cups flour. Beat until smooth. Stir in enough of remaining flour to make dough easy to handle. *(contd.)*

St. Lucia Buns (contd.)

Turn dough onto lightly floured surface; knead until smooth. Place in greased bowl, cover and let rise until doubled. Punch down dough; divide into 24 parts. Shape each piece into an S-shaped rope; curve both ends into a coil. Place a raisin in the center of each coil. Place rolls on greased cookie sheet. Brush tops lightly with margarine; let rise until doubled. Mix 1 egg and 1 tablespoon water; brush buns lightly. Sprinkle with 2 tablespoons sugar. Bake at 350° for 15-20 minutes. Makes 24 buns.

NOTE: Some Swedish cooks leave out the cardamom when saffron is used.

Gustavus Adolphus College Food Service, St. Peter, Minnesota
from Superbly Swedish: Recipes and Traditions

Shrove Tuesday Buns

Semlor

Dough:
1 pkg. dry yeast
1/4 cup warm water
2/3 cup milk
1/4 cup sugar
1/4 tsp. salt
1/3 cup butter (soft)
2 1/2 to 3 cups flour, divided
1 egg for glazing, beaten well

Filling:
8 oz. almond paste
3/4 cup whipping cream
1/2 tsp. vanilla
powdered sugar

To prepare dough: stir yeast into water in large bowl. Let sit for a couple minutes. Add milk, sugar, salt and butter. Add 1 1/2 cups flour. Beat dough until shiny and smooth. Add flour until stiff. Knead until smooth.

-103-

(contd.)

Shrove Tuesday Buns   *(contd.)*

Place dough in a bowl; cover with a cloth, and let rise in warm area for about 1 hour. Divide dough into 4 parts, and then divide each part again 3-4 times. Shape into round buns on floured board. Place on greased baking sheet and let rise for about 1 hour. Brush buns with beaten egg, and bake at 400° for 10-13 minutes or until golden brown. Cool on rack.

To fill: cut all of the almond paste into as many slices as you have buns. Whip cream; add vanilla, and whip again until cream is stiff. Slit buns horizontally about 1/3 from the top, but do not slice completely through. Put the almond paste in the slit and spoon in whipped cream until the lid of bun stays open. Sprinkle with powdered sugar and serve. Makes 12 to 16 buns.

Kerstin says: "Many times the 'semlor' are served as dessert in a bowl with warm milk added."

Coffee Bread   Vetebröd

Dough:
12 Tbs. butter or margarine
2 cups milk
2 oz. yeast
3/4 cup sugar
1 tsp. ground cardamom
6 cups flour

Filling:
6 Tbs. butter or margarine
1/2 cup sugar
1/2 Tbs. cinnamon or 2 oz. ground nuts

Topping:
1 egg, beaten
pearl sugar

To prepare dough: melt butter in saucepan. Add milk and remove from heat. Crumble yeast into large mixing bowl; add sugar, cardamom and milk mixture. Stir in the flour a little at a time and work dough until smooth and shiny.

(contd.)

Coffee Bread *(contd.)*

Cover and let rise for 10 minutes. Turn onto board and knead well. Divide into parts and shape into rolls or loaves. Let rise on baking sheet until doubled. Brush with beaten egg and sprinkle with pearl sugar. Bake rolls at 425° for 5-10 minutes; bake loaves at 400° for 15-20 minutes. Do not overbrown.

*If making loaves, divide dough into 4 parts and roll each piece to a 14x8-inch rectangle. Spread with filling made by mixing together butter, sugar and cinnamon or ground nuts. Roll up from long side and place on baking sheet. Clip each loaf at 1-inch intervals with scissors held perpendicular to the top. Pull sections out to the sides, alternately, to expose the pattern of the filling. Bake as directed above.

(contd.)

Coffee Bread *(contd.)*

VARIATIONS

To make rolls (*bullar*): divide dough into 4 parts and roll each piece to a 14x8-inch rectangle, as above. Spread with filling and roll up from long side; slice each loaf into 1 1/2-inch thick rounds. Place rounds, cut side up, on baking sheet. Let rise and bake as directed above.

For buttercake: Make rolls as for *bullar*, but slice the rolls into rounds 1 1/4 inches thick. Place rounds, cut side up, into buttered cake pan, about 3/4 inch apart. Let rise and bake as above.

For saffron buns: To the basic dough, add 2 Tbs. additional butter, 1 beaten egg and 1/2 tsp. ground saffron with the milk mixture. Pinch off small pieces of the kneaded dough, roll into 8-inch sticks and curl into "s" or other shapes.

 (contd.)

Coffee Bread *(contd.)*

Place a raisin in each curl. Let rise and brush with beaten egg before baking. Do not use filling or pearl sugar topping.

For Fat Tuesday buns *(fettisdagsbullar* **or** *semlor***):** use half of the basic dough recipe. Pinch off small pieces of the kneaded dough and roll into smooth balls. Let rise and brush with beaten egg, but omit pearl sugar. Bake as above. After baking, let cool covered with a tea towel. Cut a lid off the top of each bun and hollow out inside. Mix these crumbs with 3 Tbs. sugar, 3/4 cup chopped nuts and 1 1/2 cups whipping cream, whipped. Fill the buns with this mixture, replace lids, and dust with powdered sugar. Refrigerate. May be eaten as is, or in a bowl of warm milk.

Rosemary K. Plapp
from Superbly Swedish: Recipes and Traditions

Rusks   Skorpor

2 cakes yeast or 2 pkgs. dry yeast
1/2 cup lukewarm water
flour
1 tsp. salt
1 tsp. sugar
2 cups milk, scalded
1 cup shortening

2 cups sugar
1 cup hot water
1 Tbs. salt
2 eggs, beaten
10 to 12 cups flour
3/4 tsp. ground cardamom seeds
cinnamon, sugar and cream

Dissolve yeast in lukewarm water; add a little flour, 1 teaspoon salt and 1 teaspoon sugar to make a thick paste. Set aside and let rise until bubbly. Combine milk and shortening; let cool until lukewarm. Add sugar, hot water, salt, eggs and yeast mixture. Mix well. Gradually stir in flour to make a stiff dough.

(contd.)

Rusks *(contd.)*

Add cardamom. Place in greased bowl and let rise until doubled. Punch down and knead. Shape into 20 to 24 rolls about 1 1/2x6 inches. Place rolls in two greased 13x9-inch pans. Let rise again until almost doubled. Brush with a cinnamon, sugar and cream mixture. Bake at 350° for 30-35 minutes. These rolls are very good eaten freshly baked; can be frozen, or can be made into rusks.

To make rusks, slice rolls crosswise, as one would for cinnamon rolls, about 1/4 inch thick, and place on cookie sheets. Bake at 350° for 15 minutes, turning once halfway through baking. This recipe makes 8 to 10 dozen rusks.

Suzanne says, "Every Swede loves Skorpor."

Suzanne Soderberg
from Superbly Swedish: Recipes and Traditions

Cocoa Balls   # Kokosbollar

1/2 cup margarine or butter   2 to 4 Tbs. cocoa
1/2 cup sugar   1 1/4 cups uncooked quick oatmeal
1 Tbs. vanilla sugar   shredded coconut

Combine ingredients in order and blend together thoroughly. Form into small round balls. Roll each ball in shredded coconut. Chill and store in refrigerator. An additional 1/2 to 1 cup shredded coconut can go into basic mixure.

Kerstin says: "Children love this."

Eve Busch, Uppsala, Sweden
from Superbly Swedish: Recipes and Traditions

Coffee Fingers   Finska Pinnar

1 cup butter
1/3 cup sugar
1/4 tsp. almond extract
2 1/2 cups flour

1 egg, beaten
2 Tbs. sugar
15 blanched almonds, finely chopped

Cream butter and sugar together until fluffy. Add almond extract and flour and mix thoroughly. Chill. Roll out to 1/2-inch thickness and cut into 2-inch strips. Brush with beaten egg; mix together sugar and almonds and sprinkle on top. Bake at 325° for 8-10 minutes, or until golden yellow. Makes about 55 cookies.

Elisabet Heisler, member
American Swedish Historical Museum, Philadelphia
from Superbly Swedish: Recipes and Traditions

Dream Cookies

Drömmar

1 cup butter
1 cup sugar
1 tsp. vanilla sugar

2 1/2 cups flour, sifted
1/2 tsp. ammonium carbonate
(available in drug stores)

Preheat oven to 300°. Cream the butter, sugar and vanilla sugar until light and fluffy. Mix the flour and the ammonium carbonate and add to the butter and sugar mixture. Blend well. Shape the dough into small balls and place on baking sheet. Bake for 20-25 minutes, until the cookies are pale and have a cracked surface. Makes 5 dozen.

Marianne Baeckstrom, member
American Swedish Historical Museum, Philadelphia
from Superbly Swedish: Recipes and Traditions

Lucia Gingersnaps

Luciapepparkakor

1 1/2 cups heavy cream
2 1/2 cups brown sugar
1 1/4 cups dark syrup
1 Tbs. ginger

1 Tbs. lemon rind, grated
2 Tbs. baking soda
9 cups flour

In a large bowl, whip cream, add sugar, syrup, ginger, lemon rind and baking soda. Stir 10 minutes. Add flour and work until smooth. Cover dough and leave in a cool place overnight. Turn dough onto a floured board and roll out thin. With floured cutters cut out Santa Claus, gingerbread men, houses, animals or other shapes. Brush with water and bake on greased cookie sheets in a slow oven, 250°, for 15 minutes. Leave on sheet to cool. Decorate with icing (page 115) if desired.

Elsa Maria Andersson, wife of the Swedish Consulate General, Minneapolis, Minn.
from Scandinavian Christmas: Recipes and Traditions

Icing for Lucia Gingersnaps

1/2 cup powdered sugar
1/2 egg white, beaten

Beat together powdered sugar and beaten egg white until smooth. To decorate cookies, force frosting through a fine paper tube.

from Scandinavian Christmas: Recipes and Traditions

Ginger Cookies   Pepparkakor

1 cup butter
1 1/2 cups sugar, sifted
1 Tbs. syrup
1 large egg
1 tsp. baking soda

2 tsp. cinnamon
2 tsp. ginger
1 scant tsp. cloves
2 1/2 cups sifted white flour

Cream together butter, sugar and syrup until very smooth. Add egg and beat into batter. Stir in baking soda, cinnamon, ginger and cloves. Fold in flour. Add more flour if necessary to make batter easy to handle without sticking to fingers or cookie press. Using the bar design of a cookie press, press out several long strips of batter on ungreased cookie sheets. Bake in a preheated 350° oven for 7 minutes. Strips will be a medium brown. Remove from oven and let rest for 1 minute; cut into 2-inch pieces. When cool, remove to brown paper. Store in air-tight containers. Makes 7 to 8 dozen bars. *Dorothy Fransen Liljegren*
Rock Island, Illinois

Poor Man's Cookies   Klenäter

6 eggs
6 Tbs. sugar
6 Tbs. cream

2 cups flour
1 tsp. ground cardamom seeds
fat for frying
powdered sugar

Beat eggs until lemon colored. Add sugar. Beat well. Add other ingredients to make a soft dough. Roll out thinly. Cut in long strips 1 1/4 inches wide; cut these strips diagonally about 3 inches long. Make a small slit at one end and draw the other end through. Fry in hot lard. Sprinkle with powdered sugar through a sieve. These cookies are delicious served with fruit sauce and a dollop of whipped cream.

Elizabeth (Mrs. Einar) Jaderborg
Lindsborg, Kansas

Spritz Cookies   Spritsar

1 cup butter
1 cup sugar
2 egg yolks

2 Tbs. whipping cream
1 Tbs. almond extract
3 cups flour

Cream together butter and sugar. Add egg yolks, cream and almond extract. Stir well and add flour. Be careful not to use too much flour or it will be hard to push through the spritz form. Shape with spritz cookie press on ungreased cookie sheet and bake at 350° about 8 minutes until lightly brown.

Dorothy Ossian, Stanton, Iowa
from Superbly Swedish: Recipes and Traditions

Sugar Wreaths   Sockerringar

1/2 lb. butter
3/4 cup sugar
2 eggs
3 1/4 cups flour, divided
2 tsp. ammonium carbonate crystals,
    crushed to fine powder

1/4 tsp. salt
2 tsp. cardamom
6 Tbs. cream
1 egg, whipped
1 cup pearl sugar

Cream butter, sugar and 2 eggs until light and fluffy. Mix 2 1/4 cups flour with ammonium carbonate crystals (available in drugstores), salt and cardamom, and add this to the butter mixture alternately with the cream. Using remaining flour, knead dough on board. Roll into little-finger thickness. Cut into 5-inch lengths and shape into wreaths. Brush with well-whipped egg and dip in pearl sugar. Bake at 375° for about 12 minutes.

Jenny Johnson, Minneapolis, Minnesota
from Superbly Swedish: Recipes and Traditions

Sand Tarts   Sandbakelser

1 cup butter
1 scant cup sugar
2 egg yolks
2 1/2 cups pastry flour

1 tsp. baking powder
dash almond extract
1 cup finely chopped walnuts

Cream the first three ingredients. Add remaining ingredients and mix well. Using fingers, press a small amount of dough into a couple Swedish *Sandbakelser* forms to test bake. Work dough up the sides of the little tartlet tins, using no more dough than necessary to cover tins. Bake at 350° until golden brown. Cool before removing from tins. Bake remaining dough the same way, handling tarts carefully to avoid breaking. *NOTE: Adding walnuts is American. Swedish cooks would use ground almonds. Mrs. Benson indicates she does not wash the tins, but wipes them well with a soft, dry cloth.*   Mrs. Donald (Dolores) Benson, Saint Edward, Nebraska
from Superbly Swedish: Recipes and Traditions

Rosettes

Rosetter

2 eggs
2 tsp. sugar
1/4 tsp. salt

1 cup half-and-half
1 cup flour
oil for deep frying

Beat eggs, sugar, salt and half-and-half until blended. Beat in flour, making sure the batter is smooth. Pour 2 inches of oil in medium skillet or saucepan. Heat to 375°. Heat rosette iron in hot oil for 30 seconds; shake off the excess oil. Dip at once in batter (do not let batter come over the top edge of iron). Fry in hot oil until golden brown, about 1 minute. Remove rosette from oil with a slotted spoon and drain on paper towels. Makes about 3 dozen. These may be stored in an airtight container in a cool place.

Swedish Waffles   Våfflor

1 1/3 cups plus 1 tsp.
    whipping cream, whipped
1 cup plus 1 Tbs. flour

1/3 cup ice cold water (or snow)
2 Tbs. butter, melted

Fold whipped cream into flour; add other ingredients. Let set for 1 hour. Bake in waffle iron until brown. This is a crisp waffle. Cool and serve with powdered sugar or lingonberries.

NOTE: Sour cream can be substituted for one-third of the amount of whipping cream.

Almond-Topped Cake   Toscatárta

Pastry:
2 eggs
2/3 cup sugar
4 Tbs. unsalted butter, melted
1/4 cup cream or half-and-half

1 cup flour
1 1/2 tsp. baking powder
1/2 tsp. salt
2 Tbs. bread crumbs

Almond topping:
4 Tbs. unsalted butter
1/4 cup sugar
1 Tbs. flour

1 Tbs. cream
1/3 cup blanched sliced almonds
1 tsp. vanilla

For pastry: preheat oven to 350°. Beat eggs and sugar until light and fluffy. Add cooled melted butter, cream, flour, baking powder, and salt; mix well.

 (contd.)

Almond-Topped Cake *(contd.)*

Grease a 9-inch round cake pan with butter and then sprinkle with bread crumbs; turn pan over and tap out excess crumbs. Pour batter into form. Bake cake in center of oven for about 30 minutes. The cake is done when toothpick, inserted into the middle of the cake, comes out dry.

To prepare topping: combine butter, sugar and flour in small saucepan. Stir in cream and cook over low heat, stirring constantly, for 2-3 minutes, until mixture is thick and smooth. Remove from heat. Add almonds and vanilla. When cake is done, run a knife around the edge to loosen from pan. With wire rack on top, invert cake. With another rack on bottom of cake, invert again—cake is now facing up. With spatula, spread almond topping evenly over the hot cake. Place cake, still on the rack, under broiler about 3-4 inches from heat. Broil 3-5 minutes or until top is golden brown and bubbling. Make sure topping does not burn. Serve cool.

Ambrosia Cake   Ambrosiatårta

Pastry:
3 eggs
1 cup sugar
1 cup butter
1 cup flour
 Icing:
1 Tbs. orange juice
1/3 cup powdered sugar

3/4 tsp. baking powder
butter
bread crumbs

3 Tbs. chopped candied orange peel
or chopped almonds

To prepare cake: beat eggs and sugar until white and fluffy. Stir butter until creamy and add. Sift together flour and baking powder and stir until well blended. Pour into 9-inch round cake pan that has been buttered well and sprinkle with bread crumbs. Bake at 250° for 30 minutes.

 (contd.)

Ambrosia Cake *(contd.)*

To prepare Icing: mix orange juice and powdered sugar until smooth. Spread evenly over cake and sprinkle with orange peel or almonds.

VARIATION: Sprinkle 1/4 cup rum on the cake after cooling and before frosting.

Marianne Baeckstrom, member
American Swedish Historical Museum, Philadelphia, Pennsylvania
from Superbly Swedish: Recipes and Traditions

Mazarin Cake   Mazarintårta

Pastry:

1/4 lb. unsalted butter, softened
1 1/2 tsp. sugar

2 egg yolks
1/4 tsp. salt
1 1/3 cups flour

Frangipane filling:

1/4 lb. unsalted butter, soft
1 cup almond paste, at room
    temperature

2 eggs
2 Tbs. flour
powdered sugar for decoration

For pastry: cream butter and sugar. Add egg yolks one at a time, and salt. Add flour and mix well. Shape pastry into a ball and chill for 30 minutes.

(contd.)

Mazarin Cake *(contd.)*

Roll out dough, making a circle about 12 inches in diameter and about 1/8 inch thick. Gently press the pastry into the bottom and sides of a greased 8-inch springform pan.

For filling: mix all ingredients together and beat until smooth. With a spatula, spread the filling on top of the pastry. Bake cake in the center of a preheated 325° oven until the pastry is golden brown and the filling is set, about 45-50 minutes. Let the cake cool; keep the bottom section of the springform pan; remove the sides. Place the cake on a platter and sprinkle with powdered sugar. Serve at room temperature.

Kerstin says: "A fantastic cake!"

Hanna's Apple Cake   Hannas Äppelkaka

6 to 8 apples, precooked with sugar
    or raw and thinly sliced
3 1/2 oz. butter
6 Tbs. sugar

2 egg yolks
3/4 cup ground blanched almonds
3 to 4 bitter almonds, ground
1/2 lemon, juice and grated rind
3 egg whites

Preheat oven to 400°. Place the well-drained apples in a shallow buttered baking dish. Cream butter and sugar until light and fluffy. Gradually blend in egg yolks, ground almonds, lemon juice and rind. Beat egg whites until stiff but not dry. Carefully fold into almond batter. Spread batter over apples. Bake for 15 minutes until golden. Best warm!

Lilla Sällskapet

Dream Torte   Drömtårta

Pastry:

3 eggs

2/3 cup sugar

1 tsp. baking powder

4 Tbs. potato flour

2 Tbs. cocoa

additional sugar

Filling:

1/4 lb. butter

1 cup confectioners' sugar

1 tsp. vanilla

1 egg yolk

To prepare pastry: line a 10x15-inch jelly roll pan with greased waxed paper. Preheat oven to 400°. Beat eggs and sugar until light and fluffy. Sift the dry ingredients together; add to the egg mixture and mix well. Pour into pan and bake 5 1/2 to 6 minutes, or until toothpick comes out dry. **To prepare filling:** cream all ingredients together until smooth. Turn cake onto waxed paper; remove waxed paper from top of cake and sprinkle with sugar. When cool, spread with filling. Roll together and let stand in cool place at least 2 hours before serving.

Värmland Torte — Värmlandstårta

Meringue layers:
5 egg whites
3/4 cup sugar

1 1/3 cups ground hazelnuts
3 rounded Tbs. cocoa

Butter cream frosting:
5 egg yolks
2/3 cup sugar
1/2 cup light cream

5 1/2 oz. butter
blanched almond flakes, oven toasted

For meringue layers: Preheat oven to 300°. Butter 2 removable-bottom 8-inch cake pans well and dust with flour. Beat egg whites until stiff. Carefully fold in sugar and ground hazelnuts. Sift in cocoa. *(contd.)*

Värmland Torte   *(contd.)*

Spread mixture in buttered pans. Bake for about 35 minutes, until golden brown. Remove sides and loosen meringue from bottom of pan while still somewhat warm. Let cool.

For frosting: Heat egg yolks, sugar and cream in an enameled or stainless steel pan. Stirring constantly, cook over low heat until thickened. Do not boil. Remove from heat and stir until lukewarm. Add butter, mixing well. Refrigerate until frosting reaches a stiff spreadable consistency. Spread half of frosting between the two meringue layers and the other half on top and sides. Sprinkle with oven-toasted almond flakes. Serves 8 to 10. This torte is very suitable for freezing.

VARIATION: Dalsland Torte—Add 3 1/2 ounces melted dark chocolate to the frosting mixture. *Lilla Sällskapet*

Cheese Cake   Ostkaka

2 eggs plus 1 egg yolk
1 cup sugar
1 tsp. salt
1 cup cream
2 tsp. vanilla

1/2 tsp. almond flavoring
1 rennet tablet
2 Tbs. lukewarm water
1 cup flour
1 cup milk
1 gallon lukewarm milk (100-105°)

Beat eggs, sugar, salt, cream and flavorings together. Set aside. Dissolve rennet in water. Mix flour with 1 cup milk. Add rennet and flour mixtures to warm milk. Let stand 1/2 hour, then slice through mixture carefully with a spatula about an inch apart. Let stand another 1/2 hour. Gradually drain off a scant 1/2 gallon of whey. Add egg mixture to the curds and beat. Pour into a casserole or a 13x9-inch pan and bake at 400° for 10 minutes and then at 350° for at least 1 hour or until golden brown and raised evenly. Loosen edges with a knife. *Ostkaka* will fall as it cools.

Garnet Requist, Stanton, Iowa

Cheese Cake   Ostkaka

1 Tbs. butter	5 eggs
1/2 cup sugar	1 qt. half-and-half
1 lb. dry cottage cheese	1/2 tsp. almond extract
2 Tbs. flour	3/4 cup ground almonds

Cream butter and sugar. Add cottage cheese and flour. Add eggs, half-and-half and almond extract. Beat well and add the finely ground almonds. Pour into a 12x8x2-inch well-buttered pan. Bake in waterbath (place the pan in a container with water about 1 inch deep) at 350° for about 1 hour, or until knife inserted in center comes out clean.

Swedish Custard   Vanilj Sås

3 egg yolks   1 1/2 cups heavy cream, divided
1/4 cup sugar   1 tsp. vanilla extract

In a double boiler, beat egg yolks, sugar, 1 cup cream and vanilla together. Beat constantly and cook until thick. Remove from heat. Beat vigorously until custard is cool. Whip remaining 1/2 cup cream and gently fold into custard. Chill and serve. Serves 4 to 6.

Sauce   # Kräm

3 Tbs. sugar   3 Tbs. water
2 Tbs. cornstarch   2 cups strawberry or raspberry juice

Combine sugar, cornstarch and water; mix to a smooth paste. Heat juice and add slowly to paste, stirring continuously. Cook until clear and thickened. Cool before serving.

Kerstin says: "This typical Swedish sauce is often served as a dessert over puddings, or by itself with a pitcher of cream."

Laney Wingate
from Superbly Swedish: Recipes and Traditions

Swedish Caramel Mold   Brylé Pudding

1 cup sugar, divided
6 eggs
2 cups cream

1 tsp. vanilla
1/2 cup cream, whipped

In a heavy skillet, melt 1/2 cup sugar over low heat until golden brown. Pour into a 9-inch ring mold, coating entire bottom. Beat eggs and remaining 1/2 cup sugar. Add 2 cups cream and vanilla. Pour into ring mold. Set mold in pan of hot water and bake at 325° for about 1 hour, or until knife inserted comes out clean. Cool. Dip mold quickly into pan of hot water. Unmold. Serve whipped cream over dessert.

Cream Pudding   Gräddkaka

1 1/2 cups heavy cream   1/3 cup sugar
4 eggs, separated   1/3 cup flour

Use a 1 1/2-quart round ovenproof dish, generously greased. Preheat oven to
350°. Whip cream until stiff. Add egg yolks one at a time, then the sugar and flour.
Whip egg whites until stiff. Add egg whites to mixture, gently folding in. Pour into
greased dish and bake for about 45 minutes. Serve at once with strawberry jam or
lingonberries. Serves 4 to 6.

Rice Pudding

Risgrynspudding

1/2 cup uncooked rice
4 cups whole milk
1/2 tsp. salt
2 eggs

2/3 cup sugar
1/4 tsp. nutmeg
vanilla to taste
cinnamon

Cook rice in milk with salt in a double boiler until rice is very tender and has absorbed most of the milk. Mix eggs, sugar, nutmeg and vanilla. Add a little of the hot mixture to egg mixture (to avoid curdling) and then combine all in double boiler, cooking only until thick. Sprinkle with cinnamon. Serves 6. This can be chilled, but is really best served warm.

Mrs. Wesley (Eileen)Scott, Minneapolis, Minnesota
from Superbly Swedish: Recipes and Traditions

Rice à la Malta   Ris à la Malta

2 cups cold cooked rice
1/2 cup sugar
1 cup whipping cream, whipped

1/2 cup slivered, blanched almonds
3/4 tsp. vanilla

Combine all ingredients, folding together gently. Chill completely. Serves 6 to 8. May be served with raspberry or strawberry sauce.

Kerstin says: "On Christmas Eve you have a rice pudding. The leftover rice is made into 'Rice à la Malta.' As a kid you can hardly wait for this."

Linnea B. Foster, Madison, New Jersey
from Superbly Swedish: Recipes and Tradtions

Apple Compote   Äppelkräm

5 to 7 apples
3 1/4 cups water, divided

3/4 cup to 1 cup sugar
4 Tbs. potato starch
half-and-half

Peel, quarter and core the apples. Cut into 1/4-inch slices lengthwise. Place apples in 3 cups boiling water with the sugar. Cover and simmer until apples are soft, about 3-5 minutes. Mix potato starch with 1/4 cup water. Stir into the apple mixture. Bring to a boil. Set aside to cool. Serve with half-and-half. Makes 6 servings.

Baked Apples with Golden Syrup

Stekta Äpplen med Sirap

6 to 8 apples
4 Tbs. golden or light syrup
   or maple syrup

2 Tbs. butter
well-chilled whipped cream

Preheat oven to 425°. Core apples and place in a buttered baking dish. Fill centers with syrup and drizzle a little over skins. Dot with butter. Bake for 20 minutes or until soft. Baste with syrup liquid a few times during baking. Serve with well-chilled whipped cream. Serves 3 to 4. For special occasions, heat a little brandy, pour over apples and set aflame.

Lilla Sällskapet

Swedish Baked Apples with Almond Filling

Mandelfyllda Stekta Äpplen

1 cup ground almonds
1/3 cup sugar
1/3 cup water

1 egg white
6 baking apples
3 Tbs. butter
1/3 cup bread crumbs

Blend almonds, sugar, water and egg white to a smooth paste. Peel and core apples. Brush apples with melted butter. Fill cores with almond paste. Place apples in an 8- or 9-inch baking dish. Sprinkle with bread crumbs. Bake at 350° for 30-40 minutes, or until apples are tender. Serve at room temperature with *Vanilj Sås* (page 135). Serves 6.

Tosca Apples

Tosca-Äpplen

6 apples
1/2 cup blanched almond flakes
2 oz. butter

6 Tbs. sugar
1 Tbs. flour
1 Tbs. cream or milk
cold whipped cream or vanilla ice cream

Preheat oven to 400°. Peel, halve and core the apples. Place apples, rounded side up, in a buttered baking dish. Mix remaining ingredients, except whipped cream, in a pan. Stirring often, cook over low heat for 1-2 minutes, or until thick and smooth. Pour mixture over the apples immediately. Bake for 15-20 minutes or until the apples are soft and tosca mixture is golden brown. Serve warm with cold whipped cream or vanilla ice cream.

VARIATION: Use fresh or canned pear halves, peach halves, or pineapple rings, in place of apples.   *Lilla Sällskapet*

Old-Fashioned Fruit Soup   Fruktsoppa

1 10-oz. pkg. dried fruits (prunes,
    apples and apricots)
6 1/4 cups cold water, divided
1 cinnamon stick

1 1/2 Tbs. potato starch
5 oz. concentrated fruit syrup,
   (strawberry or raspberry)

Cut the fruit into small pieces. Soak in 6 cups of cold water for 15 minutes. Add
cinnamon. Cover and simmer on low heat 10 minutes. Mix potato starch with 1/4
cup water, add to the soup and bring to a boil. Add the fruit syrup. Cool soup and
serve. Makes 4 servings.

Swedish-American Heritage

Notable Sites and Events

"The old man shows what the young man was."

Swedish proverb: from *Scandinavian Proverbs*

Looking for Swedes?

Then try: Mora, Minnesota, and most of the rest of Minnesota—*where you will also find Finns, Danes and Norwegians!* **Or go to:** Stockholm, Wisconsin, or Lindsborg, Kansas. **Or try:** Two towns with coffee pot water towers: Stanton, Iowa, and Kingsburg, California.

The Swedish Council of America has chapters in Michigan, Wisconsin, Washington, California, Illinois, Iowa, New York, Maine, Massachusetts, Connecticut, New Jersey, Colorado, Texas, Florida, North Dakota and South Dakota. There are about 7 million Swedish-American descendants living throughout the United States, principally in these locations and others listed as *Jubilee Cities* (pages 156-58) in celebration of the *Year of New Sweden '88* taking place in Wilmington, Delaware.

Swedish-American Museums and Historic Sites

The American Swedish Institute
Minneapolis, Minnesota

The Colony of Bishop Hill
Bishop Hill, Illinois

The American Swedish Historical Foundation and Museum
Philadelphia, Pennsylvania

Swedish-American Museum
Chicago, Illinois

Swedish-American Museum
Stratford, Iowa

Nordic Heritage Museum
Seattle, Washington

Chisago Lakes Area—Minnesota
Lindstrom
Taylors Falls

Gammelgården Swedish Heritage Museum
Scandia, Minnesota
Gammelkyrkan, a reconstructed log sanctuary of the Elim Lutheran Church,
built in1856, and the *Hay Lakes Museum,* housed in a restored school building,
are on the grounds.

Chisago Lakes Lutheran Church
Center City, Minnesota
Oldest Lutheran congregation in Minnesota

Kanebec County Historical Museum
Mora, Minnesota

Historic Swedish Churches

Holy Trinity
Old Swedes Church, built in 1698
Wilmington, Delaware

Gloria Dei
Old Swedes Church (1642), built in 1698-1700
Philadelphia, Pennsylvania

Jenny Lind Chapel
Built 1850-1854
Andover, Illinois

Colleges with Swedish Roots

North Park College
Chicago, Illinois

Augustana College
Rock Island, Illinois

Gustavus Adolphus College
St. Peter, Minnesota

Bethany College
Lindsborg, Kansas

Sjölunden

Sjölunden is the Swedish Language Village sponsored by the American Swedish Institute, ASI Associates, and Friends of Sjölunden in cooperation with the International Concordia Language Villages of Concordia College, Moorhead, Minnesota. The program began in 1975.

Both Swedish culture and the language are taught. Students are given Swedish names; exchange Swedish money, and live in log cabins named after provinces of Sweden. Swedish traditions for holidays, such as Midsummer's Day, St. Lucia Day, and Easter, are emphasized, as well as Swedish foods and crafts. Students learn Dala painting, woodcarving, Swedish stitchery and weaving, along with customs and popular sports.

In Honor of Swedish Americans

Carl Sandburg:

Sandburg birthplace
Galesburg, Illinois

Connemara, Sandburg home
Flat Rock, North Carolina

The Lindberghs:

Charles A. Lindbergh House
(in honor of the father of Charles Lindbergh)
Little Falls, Minnesota

Charles Lindbergh's plane,
"The Spirit of St. Louis"
National Air and Space Museum
Washington, D.C.

Mamie Doud Eisenhower:

Mamie Doud Eisenhower birthplace
Boone, Iowa

A Royal Visit

To celebrate the *Year of New Sweden '88,* Swedish King Carl XVI Gustaf and Queen Silvia scheduled a 17-day tour of the United States with visits to these American cities: Washington, D.C.; Wilmington, Del.; Philadelphia, Pa.; Trenton, N.J.; Princeton, N.J.; New York City, N.Y.; Detroit, Mich.; Chicago, Ill.; Atlanta, Ga.; Houston, Tex.; Minneapolis, Minn., and Los Angeles, Calif. Queen Silvia also scheduled a visit to Augustana College, Rock Island, Illinois. One of the highlights was a ceremony in Wilmington, featuring a re-enactment of the historic landing of the original Swedish settlers, with the King and Queen going by boat up the Christina River to the site of the 1638 landing. Many other exhibits and performances in cities and towns designated as *Jubilee Cities* were planned throughout the year as part of the celebration recognizing Sweden's contributions and impact on American culture and lifestyle.

Past Celebrations

New Sweden '88 is the third such celebration of the heritage shared by the United States and Sweden. The occasions of the 250th and 300th anniversaries of the founding of the first Swedish colony in North America were marked in 1888 and 1938. In the fall of 1888 a 250th anniversary celebration was held in Minnesota, planned by Colonel Hans Mattson, founding president of the Swedish-American Bank in Minneapolis. In 1938, Prince Bertil, uncle of the present King Gustav, represented Sweden at the tricentennial celebration in Wilmington, Delaware, after his father, Crown Prince Gustaf VI Adolf, became ill during the visit. The Prince met with President Franklin D. Roosevelt during this celebration. An important moment in the history of Stockholm, Wisconsin, came when the Burlington Zephyr made its first stop at the local train depot—just long enough for the Crown Prince, Crown Princess Louise and Prince Bertil to greet the crowd that had gathered. Prince Bertil participated in 1938 and also in the *New Sweden '88* festivities.

1638 Jubilee State / Jubilee City 1988

Cities and states selected to serve as Jubilee Cities
for the New Sweden '88 celebration include:

Arizona	Phoenix	Illinois	Bishop Hill
			Galesburg
California	Kingsburg		Rockford
	Sacramento		
	San Diego	Iowa	Decorah
	San Francisco		Des Moines
			Iowa City
Colorado	Denver		Sioux City
	Greeley		Swedesburg
	Longmont		
		Kansas	Lindsborg
Connecticut	Greater Hartford		Wichita

Massachusetts	Boston	Minnesota	New Scandia
			Roseau
Michigan	Cadillac		St. Peter
	Flint		Taylors Falls
	Greater Lansing		Warren
	Ludington		
	Manistee	Missouri	Kansas City
			Springfield
Minnesota	Almelund		St. Louis
	Atwater		
	Bemidji	Nebraska	Gothenburg
	Cambridge		Oakland
	Center City		Omaha
	Lindstrom		Stromsburg
	Moorhead		
	Mora	Nevada	Las Vegas

Jubilee Cities *(contd.)*

New Jersey	Budd Lake	Rhode Island	Entire state
New York	Jamestown	South Dakota	Dalesburg
North Dakota	Bismarck Devils Lake Fargo Grand Forks Jamestown	Texas	Austin Galveston Hutto
		Wisconsin	Eau Claire Grantsburg
Oregon	Portland		

New Sweden Farmstead

A major project of the New Sweden Company, Inc., the New Sweden Farmstead Museum, is located in historic Bridgeton, New Jersey. Seven log structures, replicas of the type built by the early Swedish-Finnish colonists, commemorate *New Sweden '88,* the 350th anniversary of the first Swedish settlement in America. The buildings include a blacksmith shop, storehouse, threshing barn, stable, a residence with an addition, a barn with an outhouse, a sauna, and a smokehouse. Many of these buildings contain authentic collections of artifacts on permanent loan to the New Sweden Company through the generosity of the Swedish people.

Formally opened by King Carl XVI Gustaf and Queen Silvia on April 14, 1988, the museum in Bridgton's 1,100 acre city park, is open from Mid-April through October. For information write: The New Sweden Farmstead, 50 East Broad Street, Bridgeton, New Jersey 08302.

The Year of New Sweden 1638-1988

Splendid Swedish Recipes is our salute to the *Year of New Sweden '88,* honoring the first Swedes who sailed aboard the *Kalmar Nyckel* to North America in 1638, landing at Fort Christina, which is now a state park at Wilmington, Delaware. These early Americans included Finnish-speaking people and the great-grandfather of John Morton, signer of the Declaration of Independence. *New Sweden '88,* a joint venture between Sweden and the United States, will be marked in many ways, one of which will be the issue of a commemorative stamp by the United States, Sweden and Finland, recognizing the founding of New Sweden.